D0365004

DUE DATE	RETURN DATE	DUE DATE	RETURN DATE

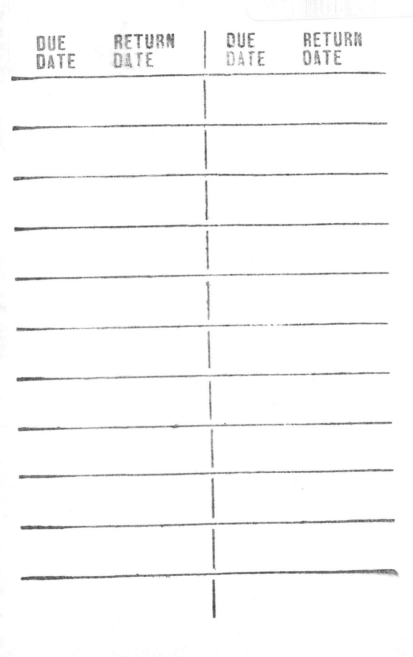

THE FRAMING OF THE CONSTITUTION
OF THE UNITED STATES

THE FRAMING OF THE
CONSTITUTION
OF THE UNITED STATES

BY

MAX FARRAND

NEW HAVEN AND LONDON
YALE UNIVERSITY PRESS

Printed in the United States of America by The Alpine Press Inc., Stoughton, Massachusetts.

ISBN: 0–300–00079–0 (paper), 0–300–00445–1 (cloth).

40   39   38   37   36   35   34   33   32

TO

A. LAWRENCE LOWELL

PREFACE

For over ten years the writer has been engaged in collecting and editing the material available upon the work of the convention that framed the constitution of the United States. Collating of texts is a wearisome and often merely a mechanical task, but in the process the editor becomes more or less familiar with the content of the documents. In the present instance the form in which the work finally shaped itself required a knowledge of the proceedings of the convention not merely as a whole, but from day to day, and it necessitated a familiarity with the thought and expressions of the individual members. When to this was added an acquaintance with the personalities of the more important delegates, a mental picture of the convention was formed which developed into a conviction as to what the delegates were trying to do and what they actually accomplished.

It is with no idea of attempting the final history of the formation of the constitution that the present book is written. If there be any truth in the epigrammatic definition that "history is past politics," it is equally true that, in the case of an institution still existing, history is present politics as well. So long as it remains the instrument under which the government of the United States is conducted, it is doubtful that any one, any American at least, can write the final word regarding the framing of our constitution.

Nor is this intended to be a complete history. It is a brief presentation of the author's personal interpretation of what took place in the federal convention. It is merely a sketch in outline, the details of which each student must fill out according to his own needs.

This book is founded upon the work the author has already referred to as edited by himself, *The Records of the Federal Convention* (New Haven, Yale University Press, 1911. 3 vols.). In the writing of it scarcely anything else has been used. The *Records* are so arranged as to render most of the citations easily found, and accordingly, with few exceptions, all footnote references have been omitted.

During the years that the work of editing and writing has been in progress, the author has presented this subject for study to classes, both graduate and undergraduate, at different institutions. To the members of those classes who have endured the exploitation of his pet theories and ideas, who have themselves suggested new points of view, and who have stimulated him to his best efforts, the author would acknowledge his grateful indebtedness.

Mr. E. Byrne Hackett, in his capacity as manager of the Yale University Press, has taken the greatest interest in the mechanical make-up of this book. In a personal and purely friendly way he also read the entire manuscript and made suggestions which resulted in its betterment. For his co-operation the author is heartily appreciative.

M. F.

New Haven, November 8, 1912.

CONTENTS

Preface vii

CHAPTER   PAGE

I. The Calling of the Federal Convention . 1
II. The Convention and Its Members . . 14
III. The Defects of the Confederation . . 42
IV. The Organization of the Convention . 54
V. The Virginia Plan 68
VI. The New Jersey Plan 84
VII. The Great Compromise 91
VIII. After the Compromise 113
IX. The Committee of Detail 124
X. Details and Compromises 134
XI. The Election of the President . . . 160
XII. Finishing the Work 176
XIII. The Completed Constitution . . . 196

APPENDIX:

I. The Articles of Confederation . . . 211
II. The Virginia Plan 225
III. The New Jersey Plan 229
IV. The Constitution of the United States . 233
V. The Amendments to the Constitution . 252
Index 261

THE FRAMING OF THE CONSTITUTION
OF THE UNITED STATES

CHAPTER I

THE CALLING OF THE FEDERAL CONVENTION

Democratic government was on trial before the world. Thirteen British colonies had asserted and established their independence because they declared the form of government under which they had been living was destructive of their "unalienable rights" of "life, liberty and the pursuit of happiness." Each of those colonies had established a government of its own, and together they had formed a union of "The United States of America" by means of certain articles of confederation. The individual state governments were proving fairly satisfactory, but the union was not. Its inadequacy had become more and more evident as the war for independence had continued and the strain of the struggle had grown harder to endure. As long as the war was in progress, the states had held together through sheer necessity; but as soon as the war was over, the selfishness of the individual states was asserting itself and the union was in danger of disintegration. The thirteen united states of America had renounced their allegiance to Great Britain, because the latter country no longer governed them well, and it now appeared as if they were unable to govern themselves. If the people of the United States were to prove their right "to assume among the Powers of the earth, the separate and equal station to which the Laws of Nature and of Nature's God entitle them," they must show themselves capable of establishing and maintaining an efficient government. To justify themselves before the world and to justify themselves in their own eyes, an effective union was essential.

The articles of confederation represented the first essay in united government that the newly independent states had made. When their congress in June, 1776, appointed a committee to draft a declaration of independence, it appointed another committee to prepare a "form of confederation," and the latter committee made its report shortly after the Declaration of Independence was adopted. The difficulty of establishing a union may be inferred from the fact that the plan submitted by the committee was the subject of intermittent discussion in congress for over a year and when the amended plan was referred to the states for ratification it was over three years before the approval of all could be secured. Although the articles of confederation were thus not formally in operation until 1781, congress seems to have followed a procedure in accordance with them, so that the experience of the confederation extended over a longer time than the official dates indicate, and really began with the establishment of independence.

The one central organ of the newly established government was a congress, which might well have been termed a congress of states: in it all the states were upon an equal footing, each with a single vote, and the delegation from each state was composed of not less than two nor more than seven members, who were appointed annually in whatever way the legislature of each state directed, who were maintained at the expense of their respective states, and who were subject to recall at any moment. To the congress thus constituted quite extensive powers were granted, but with two important limitations: none of the more important powers could be exercised "unless nine States assent to the same," which was equivalent to requiring a two-thirds vote; and when a decision had been reached there was nothing to compel the states to obedience except the mere declaration in the articles that "every State shall abide by the determinations of the United States in Congress assembled." Executive there was none, beyond the committees which the congress might establish to work under its own direction, and the only federal courts were such as congress might appoint for the trial of piracy and felony on the high seas and for determining appeals in cases of prize capture.

Under such conditions the decisions of congress were little more than recommendations. This was amply shown in the all-important matter of obtaining funds. The articles provided that the national treasury should "be supplied by the several States, in proportion to the value of all land within each State, granted to or surveyed for any person." Congress was to determine the amount of money needed and to apportion to each state its share. Congress did so, but the states honored the requisitions exactly to the extent that each saw fit, and congress had no power and no right to enforce payment. What was the result? If one may judge by the complaints that were entered, it was more profitable to disobey than to obey. In the dire straits for funds to which it found itself reduced, congress took advantage of the lack of information on land values to juggle with the estimates, so as to demand more of those states that had previously shown a willingness to pay.

The financial situation was so serious that early in 1781, before the articles had been finally ratified, congress had already proposed to the states an amendment authorizing the levy of a five per cent duty upon imports and upon goods condemned in prize cases. The amendment was agreed to by twelve states. But another weakness of the confederation was here revealed, in that the articles could only be amended with the consent of all of the thirteen states. The refusal of Rhode Island was sufficient to block a measure that was approved of by the twelve others. In 1783 congress made another attempt to obtain a revenue by requesting authority for twenty-five years to levy certain duties, and by recommending for the same term of twenty-five years that the states should contribute in proportion $1,500,000 annually, the basis of apportionment being changed from land values to numbers of population, in which three-fifths of the slaves should be counted. In three years only nine of the states had given their consent and some of those had consented in such a way as would have hampered the effectiveness of the plan. It was, however, the only relief in sight and in 1786 congress made a special appeal to the remaining states to act. Before the end of the year, all of the states had responded with the exception of New York. Again the inaction of a single state effectually blocked the will of all the others.

Matters of commerce were inseparably associated with those of finance and were at this time of equal moment. In 1784 congress made an appeal to the states in which it was said: "The situation of Commerce at this time claims the attention of the several states, and few objects of greater importance can present themselves to their Notice. The fortune of every Citizen is interested in the success thereof; for it is the constant source of wealth and incentive to industry; and the value of our produce and our land must ever rise or fall in proportion to the prosperity or adverse state of trade." The people of the United States seemed to be surprised and even resentful that their political independence had resulted in placing them outside of the British colonial system. As British colonists they had protested against the restrictions of the navigation acts, but they found those acts still more obnoxious when enforced against themselves as foreigners. Trade was adjusting itself to the new conditions and seeking new outlets, but until this had developed to a sufficient extent to make itself felt, the only possible policy, according to the prevailing conceptions of the time, was that of retaliation. The purpose of retaliation was to force other countries, and Great Britain in particular, to make concessions in favor of the United States. It was for this purpose that congress appealed to the states in 1784. It was virtually a navigation act for which power was requested and only for the term of fifteen years. All of the states responded, but with so many conflicting qualifications and conditions that the attempt was again a failure.

Pending a grant of power to congress over matters of commerce, the states acted individually. A uniform policy was necessary, and while a pretense was made of acting in unison to achieve a much desired end, it is evident that selfish motives frequently dictated what was done. Any state which enjoyed superior conditions to a neighboring state was only too apt to take advantage of that fact. Some of the states, as James Madison described it, "having no convenient ports for foreign commerce, were subject to be taxed by their neighbors, through whose ports their commerce was carried on. New Jersey, placed between Philadelphia and New York, was likened to a cask tapped at both ends; and North Carolina, between Virginia and South Carolina, to a patient bleeding at both arms." The Americans were an agricultural and a trading people. Interference with the arteries of commerce was cutting off the very life-blood of the nation, and something had to be done. The articles of confederation provided no remedy, and it was evident that amendments to that document, if presented in the ordinary way, were not likely to succeed. Some other method of procedure was necessary, and a promising way had already opened.

Virginia and Maryland had come to a working agreement regarding the navigation of Chesapeake Bay and some of its tributary waters, and those two states had requested the co-operation of Pennsylvania and Delaware. This whole proceeding was distinctly unconstitutional, for the articles of confederation specified that all such agreements must receive the consent of congress and that had not been obtained. But whether illegal or not it seemed to be an effective way of working, and in 1786 it was tried on a larger scale. Early in that year Virginia appointed commissioners "to meet such commissioners as may be appointed in the other states of the Union, at a time and place to be agreed on, to take into consideration the trade of the United States." This proposal for a general trade convention seemed to meet with approval, and the Virginia commissioners, two of whom were James Madison and Edmund Randolph, then named Annapolis and the first Monday in September, 1786, as the place and the time.

In spite of the apparently favorable attitude towards it, when the time for the convention arrived only five states were represented. At least four other states had appointed commissioners, but the individuals had not hastened their attendance. With so small a number present it was impossible for the convention to accomplish the purpose of its meeting; but with the advance in public opinion, the commissioners did not hesitate to recommend another convention of wider scope. The French representative in this country wrote home to his government, what was evidently whispered among the elect, that there was no expectation and no intention that anything should be done by the convention beyond preparing the way for another meeting, and that the report was hurried through before sufficient states were represented to be embarrassing.

Alexander Hamilton was greatly interested in this whole movement for the betterment of conditions; he took a leading part in the Annapolis trade convention, and is supposed to have drafted its report. Whether or not there is any truth in the assertion above, that Hamilton thought it advisable to conceal his purposes, there is no doubt that the Annapolis convention was an all-important step in the progress of reform. Its recommendation was the direct occasion of the gathering of the convention that framed the constitution of the United States.

The recommendation, which the Annapolis delegates made, took the form of a report to the legislatures of their respective states, in which they referred to but did not enumerate "important defects in the System of the Fœderal Government," which were "of a nature so serious as,

. . . to render the situation of the United States, delicate and critical, calling for an exertion of the united Virtues and Wisdom of all the Members of the Confederacy." They were accordingly "of Opinion, that a Convention of Deputies from the different States, for the special and sole purpose of entering into this investigation [of determining what the defects were] and digesting a Plan for supplying such defects" was the best method of procedure. To give their proposal a more concrete form they finally suggested that their respective states should "use their endeavours to procure the concurrence of the other States, in the Appointment of Commissioners to meet at Philadelphia on the second Monday in May next, to take into Consideration the situation of the United States to devise such further Provisions as shall appear to them necessary to render the Constitution of the Fœderal Government adequate to the exigencies of the Union; and to report such an Act for that purpose to the United States in Congress Assembled, as when 'agreed to by them and afterwards confirmed by the Legislatures of every State' will effectually provide for the same."

The Virginia legislature acted promptly upon this recommendation and, as no method was specified, very naturally followed its practice in providing for the representation of the state in congress by appointing a similar delegation to go to Philadelphia. This precedent of appointing a delegation similar to its delegation in congress was followed by the other states. New Jersey took action almost at the same time as Virginia, and actually named her deputies in advance of that state. Within a few weeks, Pennsylvania, North Carolina, Delaware, and Georgia had also made appointments. As yet congress had not given its approval of the plan, and many people in the United States doubted that such a meeting could accomplish anything without having the sanction of the only body authorized by the articles of confederation to propose amendments. This last obstacle was removed, however, on February 21, 1787, when congress adopted a resolution in favor of a convention, and embodied the suggestions of the Annapolis report as to time and place.

Before the time fixed for the meeting of the Philadelphia convention, or shortly after that date, all of the other states had appointed deputies with the exception of New Hampshire and Rhode Island. New Hampshire was favorably disposed towards the meeting, but owing to local conditions failed to act before the convention was well under way. Its deputies, however, arrived in time to share in some of the most important proceedings. Rhode Island alone refused to take part, though a letter signed by a committee of merchants, tradesmen, and others, was sent to the convention expressing their regret at Rhode Island's failure to be represented and pledging their influence to have the result of the deliberations approved and adopted by the state.

The federal convention was thus summoned to meet in Philadelphia on the second Monday of May, 1787. It was authorized by congress, and it was shared in by twelve of the thirteen states comprising the confederation. Whatever complex of causes there may have been, the sequence of events resulting in this convention was, as outlined, the apparent impossibility of obtaining from the states the necessary amendments to vest in congress adequate powers in taxation and commerce, the calling of a trade convention, and then the calling of a general convention.

NOTE

THE THIRTEEN UNITED STATES WITH DATES OF THEIR FIRST CONSTITUTIONS

New Hampshire . . .	1776
South Carolina	1776
Rhode Island[1]	1776
Virginia	1776
New Jersey	1776
Delaware	1776
Pennsylvania	1776
Connecticut[2]	1776
Maryland	1776
North Carolina	1776
Georgia	1777
New York	1777
Massachusetts	1780

[1] Continued under charter of 1663.
[2] Continued under charter of 1662.

CHAPTER II

THE CONVENTION AND ITS
MEMBERS

VIRGINIA had been the first state to act upon the suggestion of the Annapolis report and it followed its practice in providing for the state's representation in congress. The appointment of seven deputies was ordered by joint ballot of both houses of the legislature, any three of whom were authorized to join with the deputies from other states "in devising and discussing all such Alterations and farther Provisions as may be necessary to render the Fœderal Constitution adequate to the Exigencies of the Union and in reporting such an Act for that purpose to the United States in Congress as when agreed to by them and duly confirmed by the several States will effectually provide for the same." It will be noticed that the wording of this appointment is very similar to that in the Annapolis report. The modifications are slight and if they have any significance, they indicate a willingness on the part of Virginia to render the work of the convention effective.

At the head of its deputation Virginia placed the leading citizen of the state, and the leading citizen of the United States as well, George Washington. He was then fifty-five years of age and at the height of his popularity. The successful outcome of the Revolution had effectually silenced all criticism of his conduct of the war and his retirement to Mount Vernon had appealed to the popular imagination. The gratitude of a people, as yet unmixed with envy and undiminished by the rancor of party bitterness, placed him upon the very pinnacle of public favor. The feeling towards him was one of devotion, almost of awe and reverence. His presence in the convention was felt to be essential to the success of its work and, much against his will, Washington was finally persuaded to accept the appointment.

Patrick Henry was the second on the list, but declined to serve. The next year he came out in bitter opposition to the constitution. Dr. Grigsby, the historian of the Virginia state convention of 1788, reports that when asked why he had not taken his seat in the federal convention and helped to make "a good Constitution instead of staying at home and abusing the work of his patriotic compeers? Henry, with that magical power of acting in which he excelled all his contemporaries, and which before a popular assembly was irresistible, replied: 'I smelt a Rat.' " To the vacancy caused by Henry's

refusal the governor appointed Dr. James
McClurg, a learned physician, but with little
experience in public life. Richard Henry Lee
and Thomas Nelson were also elected but
declined to serve.

The next on Virginia's list was the governor
of the state, Edmund Randolph. Thirty-four
years old, portly and nearly six feet tall, he had a
remarkably handsome face with large and brilliant dark eyes. His manners were dignified
and polished. He usually showed an excellent
command of language and appeared well in
debate. As a leader he was wanting in decision,
as a figurehead he was splendid.

Then came John Blair, whose learning
and ability had made him a judge in the
highest courts of Virginia. Courteous, gentle-
mannered, and particular in dress, he was, as
one of his fellow-delegates, Pierce of Georgia,
remarked, "one of the most respectable Men in
Virginia, both on account of his Family as well
as fortune."[1] He was no orator, and he never
played a conspicuous part, "but his good sense,
and most excellent principles, compensate for
other deficiencies."

[1] William Pierce of Georgia left a series of brief character
sketches or notes of his fellow-delegates, evidently jotted down
at the time. Original, and very interesting, they have been of
material service in the preparation of this chapter. Most of the
direct quotations are taken therefrom.

James Madison was the most inconspicuous of the Virginia delegation. He was slender, under medium height, retiring in manner and "always dressed in black." He was a student of history, methodical and indefatigable. But Madison took an active part in public affairs, and at thirty-six he had held various official positions in Virginia and twice represented his state in congress. Pierce described him by saying that "every Person seems to acknowledge his greatness. He blends together the profound politician with the Scholar. . . . and tho' he cannot be called an Orator, he is a most agreeable, eloquent and convincing Speaker. . . . The affairs of the United States, he perhaps, has the most correct knowledge of, of any man in the Union." Madison was essentially a scholar in politics.

Two notable men completed this remarkable deputation. One was George Wythe, fifty-five years old, a signer of the Declaration of Independence, "the famous professor of law" at William and Mary, and for ten years a chancellor of the state. The other was George Mason, the author of the Virginia Bill of Rights and at sixty-two the rival of Patrick Henry in popular estimation as the champion of the rights of the people and of the states. According to Madison, he possessed "the greatest talents for debate of any man he had ever seen or heard speak." He was a gentleman of the old school, courtly but self-willed.

NEW JERSEY, the next state to act, appointed four commissioners and later increased the number to six, any three of whom were to represent the state "for the purpose of taking into Consideration the state of the Union, as to Trade and other important Objects, and of devising such other Provisions as shall appear to be necessary to render the Constitution of the Federal Government adequate to the exigencies thereof."

The delegation from this state was hardly equal to that of Virginia either in reputation or ability, although it contained some notable men. David Brearley, forty-one years old, was the chief justice of the state. He was an able, though not a brilliant man, and of a temperament and character that won and retained for him the complete respect of the people. William C. Houston, for twelve years a professor of mathematics at Princeton, admitted to the bar after he was forty, had been appointed clerk of the state supreme court, and had been one of the delegates to the Annapolis convention. William Paterson, born at sea of Irish parents, now a man of a little over forty and another of the delegates to Annapolis, had been a member of the continental congress. He had also been attorney-general of his state for eleven years. Short in stature, unassuming in appearance and manner, Paterson was all the more astonishing in debate, where he revealed wide knowledge and great ability.

William Livingston, the governor of the state, who was also noted as a wit and writer, was appointed by the legislature in the place of John Neilson, who had declined. He was independent in action as well as in speech, but he was sufficiently admired and respected to have been regularly re-elected governor of his state since the beginning of the Revolution. In person he was so tall and thin that he was frequently referred to as the "whipping post." Pierce admired him as being "about sixty years old, and remarkably healthy," but he criticized him for seeming "rather to indulge a sportiveness of wit, than a strength of thinking."

Abraham Clark, who was appointed at this time, never attended, and the delegation was completed with the selection of Captain Jonathan Dayton, who had served with distinction in the Revolution. At twenty-seven, he was one of the youngest men appointed, and occasionally revealed a hasty temper which was characteristic of him but was not in harmony with the general tone of the convention. He was a member of the state legislature, but he and Brearley were the only attending delegates from New Jersey who had not served in congress.

PENNSYLVANIA in appointing seven deputies, any four of whom were authorized to represent the state, specifically cited Virginia's act and vested its representatives with powers that were phrased like those of Virginia.

At the head of the delegation was General Thomas Mifflin, a former member and president of congress. At forty-three he was still extremely popular in spite of the fact that he had been a member of the cabal against Washington in favor of Gates. Next came "Bob" Morris, large, florid, and pleasantly impressive. Although foreign-born, he had served his adopted country well as a member of congress, a signer of the Declaration of Independence, and as the financier of the Revolution. Much was expected of him in the convention because of the financial situation and the definite ideas he was known to possess upon that subject, and also because of the reputation that "when he speaks in the Assembly of Pennsylvania, he bears down all before him."

The less conspicuous members of the Pennsylvania delegation, although they had all been in congress, were: George Clymer, a signer of the Declaration of Independence, able but extremely diffident, and never heard to speak ill of anyone;

Jared Ingersoll, the ablest jury lawyer in Philadelphia; and Thomas Fitzsimons, of Irish birth,
now a prominent and successful merchant in
Philadelphia.

James Wilson was the strongest member of
this delegation and Washington considered him
to be one of the strongest men in the convention.
Born and educated in Scotland, he came to
America when twenty-three years old. He had
served several times in congress, and had been
one of the signers of the Declaration of Independence. At forty-five he was regarded as one
of the ablest lawyers in America. Tall and large
featured, his nearsightedness compelling the use
of glasses and adding a touch of sternness to his
appearance, he had won the respect of many but
the affection of few. "James the Caledonian,"
as he was sometimes called, was rather a tribute
to his character and his oratory than a mark of
popularity.

Gouverneur Morris was probably the most
brilliant member of the Pennsylvania delegation
and of the convention as well. Sharp-witted,
clever, startling in his audacity, and with a won-
derful command of language, he was admired
more than he was trusted, for he was inconsistent
and he was suspected of being lax in morals as
well as lacking in principles. A crippled arm
and a wooden leg might detract from his per-

sonal appearance, but they could not suppress his spirit. This story is told in various forms and doubtless has a foundation of truth, and the version which attaches the incident to the federal convention is as good as another: Morris was one day boasting in the presence of several delegates that he was afraid of no one, when Hamilton offered to bet him a dinner and wine for the company that he would not dare to treat General Washington familiarly by slapping him on the shoulder. Hamilton lost the bet, but Morris in recounting his experience said that he had never won a bet which cost him so dearly, and Washington had only "looked at" him.

Shortly before the convention met, by a special act of the legislature, the aged Benjamin Franklin, president of the state, was added to the Pennsylvania delegation. "The American Socrates" was second only to Washington in reputation and popularity, but at eighty-one his powers were failing. Pierce notes with apparent surprise that "he does not shine much in public Council,—he is no Speaker, nor does he seem to let politics engage his attention. He is, however, a most extraordinary Man, and tells a story in a style more engaging than anything I ever heard."

NORTH CAROLINA appointed five deputies, any three of whom were to represent the state, and who were authorized "to discuss and decide upon the most effectual means to remove the defects of our Fœderal Union, and to procure the enlarged Purposes which it was intended to effect." This delegation was not the equal of those that had been previously appointed from the other states. Governor Richard Caswell and Willie Jones declined commissions. When substitutes had been appointed, the head of the delegation was Ex-Governor Alexander Martin. He had been dismissed from the army for cowardice in the battle of Germantown, but he had shown himself to be a good politician in that he had succeeded, in spite of his disgrace, in being governor of his state from 1782 to 1785.

Next came William R. Davie. Not yet thirty years old and one of the youngest members in the convention, with a winning personality, he was popular but not prominent. About the middle of June various Philadelphia papers gave "an exact list of the members of the convention." First came those who had risen to the title of "His Excellency," the "Honorable Governor," etc. Then were given those who were or had been "honorable Delegates to Congress." Lastly came those who were classified as "the following respectable Characters." Davie was essentially in this class.

Richard D. Spaight was also under thirty,

and if he had not been a delegate to congress, would doubtless have been classed among the "respectable characters." Pierce described him as "a worthy man, of some abilities, and fortune." Doctor Hugh Williamson had been a preacher and then a professor of mathematics in the college of Philadelphia before taking up the study of medicine. He was eccentric but good-humored, and without being a good speaker he was very fond of debating. One of his contemporaries reported that it was hard to know his character well, it was even possible that he hadn't any. Perhaps Pierce characterized him aptly when he said that "in his manners there is a strong trait of the Gentleman." William Blount, twice a delegate to congress, faithful, but without "any of those talents that make men shine . . . plain, honest and sincere," completed this mediocre delegation.

The DELAWARE commission was copied after those of Pennsylvania and Virginia, but with the important proviso "that such Alterations or further Provisions, or any of them, do not extend to that part of the Fifth Article of the Confederation . . . which declares that 'In determining Questions in the United States in Congress Assembled each State shall have one Vote.'" Five deputies were appointed, any three of whom were to represent the state.

At the head of the delegation was George Read, then in his fifty-fourth year. Short, slight, and with an appearance of physical weakness, he made but a poor impression as a speaker, although he had great ability as a lawyer. He commanded the implicit confidence of his state, which among other capacities he had represented in congress, and as a signer of the Declaration of Independence, and in the Annapolis convention.

Gunning Bedford had a great reputation as an advocate, but though an eloquent, he was also a nervous speaker and apt to be hasty and impetuous. His epitaph reads that "his form was goodly," which is a euphemistic way of describing what Pierce called being "very corpulant," and to Pierce he did not look his forty years. He, too, had represented his state in congress.

The most noted of the Delaware deputation was John Dickinson, author of the "Farmer's Letters," and chairman of the committee of congress that framed the articles of confederation. He was able, scholarly, and sincere, but nervous, sensitive, and cautious to the verge of timidity. His refusal to sign the Declaration of Independence had cost him his popularity. Though he was afterwards returned to congress and became president successively of Delaware and Pennsylvania, he never succeeded in completely regaining the public confidence. A shadow of mistrust was always visible. He appeared older than his fifty-five years would warrant.

Richard Bassett and Jacob Broom completed the delegation. They were about the same age of thirty-five, and came under the classification of "respectable characters." Pierce regarded the former with curiosity or misgiving as "a religious enthusiast, lately turned Methodist," but he commended him, and Broom as well, for having sense enough not to talk in the convention.

GEORGIA also modeled its commission on that of Virginia and appointed six commissioners, any two of whom were to represent the state. Ex-Governor George Walton and Nathaniel Pendleton either declined or failed to attend and the delegation was thus reduced to four.

William Few was a self-made man who had been admitted to the bar, and his colleague Pierce thought that "from application" he had "acquired some knowledge of legal matters." He had done more than that, however, and though socially he was at a disadvantage he was evidently well thought of in his state, for he was a member of the state legislature and twice had been a delegate to congress.

Abraham Baldwin, thirty-three years old, was the ablest member of the delegation. Born in

Connecticut, educated at Yale and a tutor there for several years, he had served during the Revolution as a chaplain in the army. After the war he had moved to Georgia, where he was admitted to the bar and became a member of the state legislature. He originated and put through the plan for the University of Georgia and then became its president. He had twice been a member of congress.

William Pierce, whose comments on his fellow delegates have been so frequently quoted, was nearly fifty years old. He had served with distinction during the Revolution, and was at this time a delegate to congress. Although he did not attempt to describe his own character, but left it for "those who may choose to speculate on it, to consider it in any light that their fancy or imagination may depict," he was evidently blessed with a sense of humor.

The last of the delegation was William Houstoun, who was admitted by Pierce to be of good family and to have been well educated in England. His next comment, however, is scathing: "Nature seems to have done more for his corporeal than mental powers. His Person is striking, but his mind very little improved with useful or elegant knowledge."

The six states that have been considered were acting on their own responsibility. The commissions they had issued all provided for a revision of the articles of confederation, but congress was the only body authorized to propose amendments to that document, and congress had made no move. When it became evident that the convention had sufficient support to render its existence a certainty, it seemed wise to congress to approve what could not be helped. Accordingly, on February 21, 1787, congress declared:

Whereas there is provision in the Articles of Confederation and perpetual Union, for making alterations therein, . . . And whereas experience hath evinced, that there are defects in the present Confederation, as a mean to remedy which, several of the States . . . have suggested a convention for the purposes expressed in the following Resolution. . . .

Resolved, That in the opinion of Congress, it is expedient, that on the second Monday in May next, a Convention of Delegates, who shall have been appointed by the several States, be held at Philadelphia, for the sole and express purpose of revising the Articles of Confederation, and reporting to Congress and the several Legislatures, such alterations and provisions therein, as shall, when agreed to in Congress, and confirmed by the States, render the federal Constitution adequate to the exigencies of Government, and the preservation of the Union.

NEW YORK seems to have been responsible for this resolution, which was introduced in congress in accordance with specific instructions to its delegates by that state. The one serious obstacle to the convention being thus removed, New York promptly joined the other states, and using the words of the resolution of congress, appointed three delegates.

The first of these was Robert Yates, an able judge of the state supreme court. He was nearly fifty years old, had been a member of the New York provincial congress and had served on the committee that framed the state constitution of 1777. John Lansing was a young lawyer of moderate ability, but he evidently was something of a politician, for he had been a member of the state house of representatives, the mayor of Albany, and a delegate to congress.

The third and ablest of this delegation was Alexander Hamilton, who was one of the smallest men physically and one of the biggest intellectually who attended the convention. Only thirty years old, his reputation was already established by what he had done in the Revolution, in his state legislature, in the continental congress, and in the Annapolis convention. The logic of his arguments was convincing, but he was not a great speaker, except on the few occasions when his feelings overmastered his self-consciousness. He was too arrogant and overbearing to be popular, but he was respected for his ability and admired for his originality and his daring.

SOUTH CAROLINA followed promptly after New York and appointed four deputies, two of whom might represent the state "in devising and discussing all such Alterations, Clauses, Articles and Provisions, as may be thought necessary to render the Fœderal Constitution entirely adequate to the actual Situation and future good Government of the confederated States."

At the head of the delegation was the Irish-American, John Rutledge, who was regarded as the great orator of his day, and as "one of the claims to fame of South Carolina." He was approaching fifty and he had been a member of congress, governor of his state, and chancellor also. A man of unquestioned ability, noted for his quick wit and for his boldness and decision, whose temper was proud and imperious, he was distinctly a person to be reckoned with. Outwardly he was possessed of considerable means, but it was rumored that his debts exceeded his fortune.

Charles Pinckney, at twenty-nine, was the youngest member of the delegation and one of the youngest men in the convention, and he must have appeared to be still younger, for Pierce speaks of him as only "twenty-four." Rather superficial but brilliant, with a high opinion of his own ability and with extraordinary conversational powers, it is little wonder that he pushed himself forward, and it is not surprising that he seems occasionally to have been sharply snubbed by his elders.

Charles Cotesworth Pinckney, a cousin nearly ten years older, was a man of a very different type. He had risen to the rank of brigadier-general during the Revolution, but he had been educated at Oxford and he was now a lawyer of promise, and a great social favorite. When he spoke it was with conviction, and what he said was listened to with respect.

Pierce Butler, of noble birth and inordinately vain of it, had served in America as an officer in the British army. He was a man of fortune and having sold his commission and settled in this country he had become very popular. At forty-three, he was a member of the South Carolina legislature and had just been elected to congress.

Henry Laurens, a former president of congress, either declined an appointment or failed to attend.

Massachusetts cited the resolution of congress, and commissioned five delegates, any three of whom were authorized to represent the state "for the purposes aforesaid." Francis Dana, one of the appointees, did not accept or at least did not attend the convention and the delegation was reduced to four.

Elbridge Gerry was small in person, but a prominent figure in state politics. At forty-three he had twice been a delegate to congress, and was one of the signers of the Declaration of Independence and of the articles of confederation. He was a successful merchant and greatly interested in questions of commerce and finance. Serenely confident of his own judgment, and unable always to distinguish between what was essential and what was of minor importance, his decisions and subsequent actions sometimes seemed unreasonable, not to say erratic.

Nathaniel Gorham, twice a delegate to congress and president of that body during his second term, had left the president's chair to attend the convention. He was a man of good sense rather than great ability, but he stood "high in reputation, and much in the esteem of his Country-men." Pierce further said of him in his fiftieth year that he was "rather lusty, and has an agreeable and pleasing manner."

Rufus King, somewhat over medium height, was an unusually handsome man and with great personal charm. Of marked ability, and an eloquent speaker with a sweet, clear voice, it is no wonder that "ranked among the Luminaries of the present Age" he should be regarded as one of the coming men of the new nation. He had been opposed to any radical reform of the confederation, but convinced of his error he joined heartily in the work of the convention and, as might be supposed, his support was as heartily welcomed.

Caleb Strong, forty-two years old, tall and angular, was rather unprepossessing in appearance. Solid rather than brilliant, plain in speech and manner, and of sterling integrity, he was highly esteemed by his colleagues and was a good representative of the country people of Massachusetts.

CONNECTICUT also specifically referred to the action of congress and appointed three delegates, any one of whom might represent the state "for the purposes mentioned." But as if in further explanation the act goes on to say "and to discuss upon such Alterations and Provisions agreeable to the general principles of Republican Government as they shall think proper to render the federal Constitution adequate to the exigencies of Government and the preservation of the Union." Erastus Wolcott having declined to serve, the commission consisted of Johnson, Sherman and Ellsworth.

William Samuel Johnson was sixty years of age and was regarded as one of the most learned men in this country; having received the degree of Doctor of Laws from Oxford, he was always addressed and referred to as "Doctor" Johnson. A lawyer and judge who, in spite of his luke-warmness during the Revolution, was greatly respected, he had just been elected president of Columbia College. Gentle-mannered, and almost affectionate in his way of addressing acquaintances, he was loved as well as respected. Whenever he spoke, he was accorded the most careful attention.

Roger Sherman, the mayor of New Haven, was at sixty-six one of the older men in the convention. Tall, awkward, and almost uncouth, he was apt to be misjudged at first sight, for he was a man of ability and of great practical wisdom. Shoemaker, almanack-maker, lawyer, and judge had been the successive stages of his progress. "An able politician, and extremely artful in accomplishing any particular object;—it is remarked that he seldom fails." Another of his contemporaries wrote: "he is as cunning as the Devil, and if you attack him, you ought to know him well; he is not easily managed, but if he suspects you are trying to take him in, you may as well catch an Eel by the tail." He had been a member of congress and a signer of the Declaration of Independence and of the articles of confederation.

Oliver Ellsworth, forty-two years old, was a judge of the state supreme court who was greatly "respected for his integrity, and venerated for his abilities." An eloquent speaker and an able debater, he made an excellent third in this rather remarkable trio. A few months later the French *chargé d'affaires* in a report to his government spoke of Ellsworth and Sherman as typical of Connecticut, and went on to say: "The people of this state generally have a national character not commonly found in other parts of the country. They come nearer to republican simplicity: without being rich they are all in easy circumstances."

MARYLAND, in phrases very similar to those of the original Virginia act, commissioned five deputies, but owing to the exigencies of local politics the final appointments were not made until two weeks after the date set for the opening of the convention. It was said that the first men chosen by the legislature refused the appointment, because it would involve absence from the state when their presence and influence were needed to restrain a widespread movement for an issue of paper money. At any rate, Charles Carroll of Carrollton, Gabriel Duvall, Robert Hanson Harrison, Thomas Sim Lee, and Thomas Stone were elected but declined to serve, and the delegation finally appointed was regarded as inferior.

Dr. James McHenry, born in Ireland, had been a surgeon during the Revolution and had

become secretary to the commander-in-chief and
Washington's friend and adviser. He had since
been a member of the state senate and a delegate
to congress. A man of only moderate ability,
he had at thirty-five achieved a prominence
somewhat beyond his merit.

Daniel of St. Thomas Jenifer, sixty-four years
old, was a man of means and of some prominence
in his state. He had been a delegate to congress,
and one of the commissioners from Maryland to
meet with Virginia in the Chesapeake-Potomac
controversy. "He is always in good humour,
and never fails to make his company pleased with
him. He sits silent in the Senate, and seems to
be conscious that he is no politician. From his
long continuance in single life, no doubt but he
has made the vow of celibacy."

Daniel Carroll and John Francis Mercer were
two younger men, the one just over and the other
under thirty, of large means, who were rising
into political prominence in the state. Both had
been delegates to congress.

Luther Martin was an able lawyer, forty-three
years old, who had been a delegate to congress
and had been appointed attorney-general of
Maryland. His career in politics was ascribed to
the influence of undesirable interests, and it was
said that he was sent to the federal convention for
the purpose of opposing the establishment of a

strong national government. He was a tiresome speaker, perhaps a trait that he carried over from his school-teaching days, and that fact together with the suspicion attaching to his motives did not insure him a cordial reception.

NEW HAMPSHIRE, according to common report, failed to act because of lack of funds to meet the expenses of its delegates, and the situation was not relieved until John Langdon offered to pay all expenses out of his private purse. When action finally was taken late in June, it seemed necessary to defend or explain the state's position. Accordingly in the act appointing commissioners, a somewhat elaborate preamble was adopted, recognizing the necessity of enlarging the powers of congress, and declaring the unselfishness of the state and its willingness to make every concession to the safety and happiness of the whole. Four deputies were accordingly named, any two of whom were authorized to represent the state, "to discuss and decide upon the most effectual means to remedy the defects of our federal Union."

Langdon, who was naturally the first man named, was not yet fifty years old and had made a large fortune in commerce. He was sometimes referred to as the Robert Morris of his state. He was eminently a practical man, of strong common sense, simple and unaffected, who had taken an active interest in the Revolution, and was "thoroughly republican in all his tendencies." He had been a member repeatedly and speaker of the state house of representatives, president of his state, and twice a delegate to congress.

Nicholas Gilman appeared to be younger than the thirty-odd years warranted. He had served during the Revolution, but the reputation he achieved seems to have been that of a self-seeker, and of one desiring to be appointed to public offices. A year before he had been elected to congress, and there on account of his youth and presumptuous airs his colleagues promptly dubbed him "Congress." Pierce said that though there was "nothing brilliant or striking" there was "something respectable and worthy in the man." But the French *chargé d'affaires*, Otto, reported to his government that his representing New Hampshire in the convention proved that there was not much from which to make a choice in that state.

John Pickering and Benjamin West were appointed but did not attend the convention, so that New Hampshire was represented by Langdon and Gilman only and they did not reach Philadelphia until the end of July.

Nearly seventy-five names have been mentioned but characterizations have been attempted

of only the fifty-five who actually attended the
convention. In some respects they were a remarkable body of men. At an average age of
forty-two or forty-three, although one-sixth
were of foreign birth, most of them had played
important parts in the drama of the Revolution,
a large majority, approximately three-fourths,
had served in congress, and practically all of
them were persons of note in their respective
states and had held important public positions.
In a time before manhood suffrage had been
accepted, when social distinctions were taken for
granted, and when privilege was the order of the
day, it was but natural that men of the ruling
class should be sent to this important convention.

Thomas Jefferson was in Paris and when he
heard of the appointments he wrote to John
Adams in London, "it really is an assembly of
demi-gods." The opinion thus expressed has
been commonly accepted since that time. The
objection to it lies in the fact that the Virginia
delegates whom Jefferson best knew were an
unusual set of men, while many of the other delegates Jefferson knew only by reputation as men
of prominence in their states. As a matter of
fact, Virginia had set the fashion, which the country approved, and to be a delegate to Philadelphia became a desired honor. Appointments
were accordingly sought and obtained in several

instances by men of political influence. In other cases appointments were due to less worthy motives, approaching what might be termed corruption. In a few cases appointments were made for convenience' sake to fill up the state delegation. A contemporary, who was frankly in the opposition, wrote: "I do not wish to detract from their merits, but I will venture to affirm, that twenty assemblies of equal number might be collected, equally respectable both in point of ability, integrity, and patriotism. Some of the characters which compose it I revere; others I consider as of small consequence, and a number are suspected of being great public defaulters, and to have been guilty of notorious peculation and fraud, with regard to public property in the hour of our distress."[1]

Doubtless the truth lies between the two opinions. Great men there were, it is true, but the convention as a whole was composed of men such as would be appointed to a similar gathering at the present time: professional men, business men, and gentlemen of leisure; patriotic statesmen and clever, scheming politicians; some trained by experience and study for the task before them, and others utterly unfit. It was essentially a representative body, taking possibly a somewhat

[1] Ford, P. L., *Pamphlets on the Constitution of the United States,* p. 115.

higher tone from the social conditions of the time, the seriousness of the crisis, and the character of the leaders.

CHAPTER III

THE DEFECTS OF THE CONFED-
ERATION

The convention had been called to meet in Philadelphia and the delegates had been appointed. For what purpose? The report of the Annapolis convention had recommended a thorough investigation into the defects of the confederation and the development of a plan for remedying those defects, and the resolution of congress had specified "for the sole and express purpose of revising the Articles of Confederation." After the experience of over a hundred years under a better system, it is easy for us to criticise the articles of confederation, for according to present-day standards they may be condemned as utterly unfit, unworkable, and even as "vicious" in principle. It is accordingly assumed that the federal convention regarded them in that light and, considering them hopeless of amendment, had started afresh to construct a new instrument of government. This is quite misleading. To the men of that time the articles of confederation appeared in no such light. His contemporaries might not have been willing to concur in Jefferson's extravagant statement that a comparison of our government with the governments of Europe "is like a comparison of heaven and hell. England, like the earth, may be allowed to take the intermediate station." Yet John Jay seemed to regard it as somewhat of a concession to admit that "our federal government has imperfections, which time and more experience will, I hope, effectually remedy." Even Washington, who of all men had suffered the most from the intolerable inefficiency of congress, had a good word to say for the government. Nor is it sufficient to accept the apology of John Marshall that, if the articles of confederation really preserved the idea of union until the nation adopted a more efficient system, "this service alone entitles that instrument to the respectful recollection of the American people." The form of government that had been established was an experiment, an attempt to solve the problem of a confederated republic, and while no one would have claimed that it was perfect most men would have agreed with Jefferson that "with all the imperfections of our present government, it is without comparison the best existing or that ever did exist."

If such was the contemporary point of view, it is evident that the wording employed in the credentials of the delegates and in the resolution of congress was no mere formal phraseology; the federal convention was really called for the "express purpose of revising the Articles of Confederation" and rendering them "adequate to the exigencies of government, and the preservation of the Union." To appreciate the work of the federal convention, it is essential to understand the task before it, as the delegates themselves comprehended it. Accordingly it is necessary to divest ourselves of preconceived ideas and prejudices due to modern misinterpretation, and to try to determine what the men of the time had in mind when they spoke of the defects "which experience hath evinced that there are . . . in the present confederation." Fortunately the problem is not a very difficult one to solve. Interest was keen, the seriousness of the country's situation was appreciated and the topic was frequently broached in correspondence between men in all sections. Some of the letters of the better known characters have been preserved to us, and from these we can ascertain fairly accurately the state of public opinion at that time.

Early criticisms of the confederation were vague; they might almost be termed desultory. But as time passed and interest increased, more careful thought was given to the subject, with a resultant increase in number and definiteness of the defects noted. But the members of the federal convention would only deal with those defects in the confederation of which they knew. The present study has therefore been limited strictly to the writings of the delegates themselves prior to the time of meeting in Philadelphia, and to the records of proceedings of which some of the members could not fail to have had knowledge, such as the journals of congress.

It has already been shown that the wretched condition of the government finances, and the unsatisfactory state of foreign and domestic trade, were responsible for the calling of the Philadelphia convention. The two subjects were closely connected. In the matter of trade a uniform policy was necessary, and that uniformity could only be obtained by granting to the central government full power over trade and commerce, both foreign and domestic. This meant of course that duties would be laid and something in the way of revenue would result. It was not expected that this would be sufficient, and if the credit of the United States was to be maintained, further and adequate powers of obtaining revenue by direct and indirect taxation must be provided. Whatever was done, some more equitable method of distributing the burden of taxation must be found than the unsatisfactory system of requisitions based upon undeterminable land values. Many thoughtful observers also saw that restrictions upon the issuing of paper money were necessary, and that something more uniform than the variable state currencies was desirable. In view of subsequent events, it is interesting to notice that Madison and Jefferson were in favor of empowering the central government to establish a national bank.

If it was exasperating to find themselves overreached in matters of international trade, it was humiliating to find themselves too weak to force the British to live up to the terms of the Treaty of Paris of 1783, and it was positively disgraceful to be unable to compel the individual states to observe the provisions of that or any other treaty that might be made.[1] Without authority to require the states to regard the principles of

[1] "There is a story, at one time commonly repeated, which illustrates the tenderness of the Virginia conscience on the subject of the repudiation of English debts during the period 1783-1789. A Scotchman, John Warden, a prominent lawyer and good classical scholar, but suspected rightly of Tory leanings during the Revolution, learning of the large minority against the repeal of laws in conflict with the treaty of 1783 (i.e., especially the laws as to the collection of debts by foreigners), caustically remarked that some of the members of the House had voted against paying for the coats on their backs. The story goes that he was summoned before the House in full session, and was compelled to beg their pardon on his knees, but as he rose, pretending to brush the dust from his knees, he pointed to the House and said audibly, with evident double meaning, 'Upon my word, a dommed dirty house it is indeed.' The Journal of the House, however, shows that the honor of the delegates was satisfied by a written assurance from Mr. Warden that he meant in no way to affront the dignity of the House or to insult any of its members." Grigsby, *Virginia Convention of 1788*, II, 86.

international law and incompetent even to punish piracy or felony on the high seas, it was truly a pitiable spectacle that the United States presented. When a contemporary who had traded with various countries could say that he found "this country held in the same light by foreign nations as a well-behaved negro is in a gentleman's family,"[2] there need be little wonder that this newly independent and sensitive people should demand reforms that would tend to dispel some of the contempt inspired abroad. The least that could be done was to establish a strong central government which should have control of all foreign relations.

These things were self-evident and there seems to have been a general unanimity of sentiment in favor of the reforms proposed. If those reforms were carried out, the situation would have been somewhat relieved, but the heart of the trouble would not have been reached. A fundamental difficulty of the union was to be found in the independence and excessive power of the individual states. Concrete instances of this are to be noticed in the matters thus far considered, which involved not merely trespassing by the states upon one another's rights, but even directly disregarding the articles of confederation. Agree-

[2] Elliot, Jonathan, *Debates in the Several State Conventions on the adoption of the Federal Constitution*, II, 34.

ments between the states were in direct contravention of that instrument. So also were the dealings with the Indians which several of the states indulged in to the detriment of any uniform policy, so important in treating with uncivilized peoples. But the blame for this encroachment upon federal authority was not to be laid at the door of the states alone. The confederation did not draw the line sharply between state and federal powers, and even in the field open to congressional action the government was frequently too weak to move. Self-preservation, rather than mere selfishness, actuated the states in some instances. But whatever justification there might be, it was greatly to be desired that a negative or some check upon state legislation should be vested in the central government.

There were some matters requiring greater uniformity of treatment and procedure than could be obtained from independent state action. Such were naturalization, bankruptcy, education, inventions, and copyright. Upon these subjects, accordingly, congress ought to be authorized to legislate. For somewhat different reasons other matters were just as clearly beyond the scope of state action and in these also the central government should be given power: To define and punish treason, to establish and exercise jurisdiction over a permanent seat of government, to hold and govern the western territory that had been ceded by the states, to provide for the establishment of new states and their admission into the union, to maintain an efficient postal service and, some said, to make internal improvements. If such fields of action were granted to the central government, the states would still be free to exercise sufficient authority in local matters. But experience had also shown that occasion might arise when a state would welcome a strong hand to assist it in preserving order within its boundaries. Shays's rebellion had taught a much needed lesson. It was not sufficient to place the state militia under some central control. The central government must be empowered to maintain an efficient army and navy to protect the states against internal disorders, as well as against external dangers. In other words, the authority of the federal government was to be effective in time of peace as well as in time of war. As a further safeguard for the states in maintaining their republican institutions, a guarantee of their constitutions and laws was believed to be essential.

Some of the more superficial observers were inclined to ascribe the difficulties of the confederation to the defective organization of the government. Montesquieu, whose writings were taken as political gospel, had shown the absolute necessity of separating the legislative, executive,

and judicial powers. There ought, therefore, to
be a separate executive which should be able to
take the initiative when occasion demanded,
which should be capable of action in foreign relations and which, either with or without a council,
might have the power of appointment and the
right of veto. There ought to be an organized
federal judiciary which should have, in addition
to that developed under the articles of confederation, jurisdiction in matters relating to foreigners
or people of other states. And the composition
of congress should be entirely changed: there
ought to be two houses and a council of revision;
the method of voting by states and of requiring
nine votes ought not to be continued; the number
of members should be greater and the people
ought to be directly represented; the sessions
should be definite and not so frequently shifted
from one place to another; attendance should be
compulsory; the members should be prohibited
from holding other offices; and the terms of office
and the compensation of members ought to be
such as would attract the best men in the country.

While recognizing the justice of these complaints and the wisdom of the reforms proposed,
more thoughtful observers realized that another
and perhaps the fundamental weakness of the
confederation was the inability of congress to
enforce its demands. Under existing conditions

it might be sufficient to render the federal constitution superior to state constitutions and to give the central government a negative or some check upon state legislation, together with the right and power of coercion. But there were a few who had studied the situation who saw that the changes desired were so far-reaching that, if they were carried out, the confederation would be transformed. They accordingly favored a central government acting directly upon the people with power to compel obedience.

The attempt to obtain amendments to the articles of confederation had taught by bitter experience that the objection of a single state was sufficient to block the will of all the others. It was evidently necessary, then, that provision should be made for amendments to the new constitution with the consent of less than the whole number of states. It was also felt that this same principle ought to be applied in the modifications proposed in the existing instrument, and those who were in favor of a government acting directly upon the people advocated as a first step in this process that the changes to be made in the constitution should be ratified by the people rather than by the state legislatures.

The points that have been noted represent roughly what the members of the convention seem to have had in mind at the time of their meeting in Philadelphia when they spoke of the defects of the confederation. It would seem probable that when such men as Madison and Hamilton attempted to point out the defects of the confederation, they would naturally include everything requisite to good government that was lacking in the articles of confederation. But the defects that have been mentioned are much more comprehensive than those which were noted by any one person. Even Madison's summary—prepared shortly before the convention met, with a long experience in the congress of the confederation and after a careful study of all the confederations known to history—is only approximately complete.

The specific task which the convention thus had before it was to remedy a series of perfectly definite defects, each of which had revealed itself in the experience of little more than ten years. It was a time when men indulged in philosophical speculation and in political theorizing, but farmers and traders are practical people, and the compelling characteristic of the framers of the constitution was hard-headed common sense. While several of the delegates in preparation for their task read quite extensively in history and government, when it came to the concrete problems before them they seldom, if ever, went outside of their own experience and observation.

THE DEFECTS OF THE CONFEDERATION

NOTE

Pelatiah Webster

Pelatiah Webster was a successful Philadelphia merchant and interested in financial questions, upon which
he had written. In 1783, he brought out a small pamphlet entitled "A Dissertation on the Political Union
and Constitution of the Thirteen United States of
America, which is necessary to their Preservation and
Happiness; humbly offered to the Public." Upon the
basis of this, extravagant claims have been made for
Webster as the "architect of the constitution." Some
of his ideas were taken directly from the articles of confederation and from the amendments that had been
proposed thereto. Some of his ideas were purely fanciful,
and were of no value whatever. Some of the things which
he foresightedly pointed out were later embodied in the
constitution, but there is not the slightest evidence that
his pamphlet or ideas—directly or indirectly—actually
affected the work of the convention. In other words, it
would seem that the constitution would have taken its
present form if the pamphlet in question had never been
written.

CHAPTER IV

THE ORGANIZATION OF THE CONVENTION

The convention had been called to meet in Philadelphia on the second Monday in May. In 1787 this fell upon the fourteenth day of the month. Upon that day, however, only a comparatively few delegates had arrived, and as this was a meeting of state deputations, it was essential that a majority of the states should be represented. Partly owing to the difficulties and slowness of travel, but partly owing to the dilatory habits developed in congress, where experience had shown that it was a waste of time to be prompt in attendance, it was not until Friday, the twenty-fifth of May, that seven states were represented and the convention could proceed to organize.

The meetings were held in the State House, and it is commonly supposed that Independence Hall was the room that was used. But Manasseh Cutler visited Philadelphia in the summer of 1787 and in his journal of July 13 he gives a brief description of the State House, in which he records that "the hall east of the aisle is employed for public business. The chamber over it is now occupied by the Continental Convention, which is now sitting." John F. Watson, in his *Annals of Philadelphia,* confirms this statement and gives the additional information that the street pavement was covered with earth that the labors of this august assembly might not be disturbed by passing traffic.[1]

The first duty was to choose a presiding officer. As president of the state in whose capitol the convention was meeting, as well as by virtue of his age and reputation, Franklin might have considered himself entitled to that honor. But when the session opened on the morning of the twenty-fifth with a majority of the states in attendance, Robert Morris on behalf of the Pennsylvania delegation formally proposed George Washington for president. Franklin himself was to have made the nomination, but as the weather was stormy he had not dared to venture out. No other names were offered, and the convention proceeded at once, but formally, to ballot upon the nomination. Washington was declared to be unanimously elected, and was formally conducted to the chair by Robert Morris and John Rutledge. With equal formality, but "in a very emphatic manner," Washington thanked the convention for the honor they had conferred upon him and in apparently stilted terms "lamented

[1] Edition of 1857, vol. I, p. 402.

his want of better qualifications" for the position. He then proposed that a secretary should be appointed.

The emoluments of the secretaryship were hardly worthy of consideration and it must have been the hope that it might lead to some future political preferment that induced several candidates to apply for the position. One of these was Major William Jackson, who had seen active service in the Revolution, had been secretary to John Laurens on his mission to France in 1781, and afterwards had been appointed assistant secretary of war. Jackson very shrewdly did some electioneering in advance by writing himself to some of the more important delegates and by getting his friends to write for him. The advantage of this was seen when the appointment was made. Jackson received the vote of five states, while the only other formal nominee, Franklin's nephew, Temple Franklin, obtained but two.

The next stage in the procedure was to read the credentials of the deputies, and it was noticed with some concern that those from Delaware were prohibited from changing the principle of the confederation of each state having an equal vote. George Mason commented on this in a letter to his son, and added that "no other State . . . hath restrained its deputies on any subject." A committee of three was then elected by ballot to prepare standing orders and rules, and after appointing a messenger and a doorkeeper the convention adjourned until Monday.

On Monday two more states were represented and the day was spent in considering the report of the committee on rules. Aside from the ordinary methods of parliamentary procedure, two things were agreed upon that are essential in understanding the working of the convention. In the first place, the whole organization of the convention was on the basis of state representation: each state having one vote, seven states making a quorum, and a majority of states present being competent to decide all questions, though the deputies of a state by simply requesting it might postpone the vote upon any question until the following day. This matter of state representation had been the subject of informal discussion during the days that elapsed while the delegates present were waiting for a quorum. The Pennsylvania delegates and Gouverneur Morris in particular urged "that the large States should unite in firmly refusing to the small States an equal vote, as unreasonable, and as enabling the small States to negative every good system of Government." The Virginia delegates, however, succeeded in stifling the project for fear that it "might beget fatal altercations between the large and small States."

In the second place, it was considered important that the delegates should be protected from criticism, and that their discussions should be free from the pressure of public opinion. Accordingly it was decided not to permit calling for the yeas and nays, and it was further ordered that "no copy be taken of any entry on the journal . . . without leave of the House," that "members only be permitted to inspect the journal," and that "nothing spoken in the House be printed, or otherwise published or communicated without leave." In other words, the sessions were to be strictly secret. We have a contemporary account revealing the excessive care taken to protect the convention from intrusion, which states that "sentries are planted without and within—to prevent any person from approaching near—who appear to be very alert in the performance of their duty."

Two days and a part of the third day were given up to the work of organization, and when the main business of the convention was begun on May 29, there were ten states represented with some forty delegates in attendance. With the exception of one adjournment of two days over the Fourth of July and another of ten days, from July 26 to August 6, to allow an important committee to prepare its report, the convention remained in continuous session (except for Sundays) until September 17. There was one week in the latter part of August when the time of adjournment was set at four o'clock, but otherwise the hours of the daily sessions seem to have been from ten in the morning to three in the afternoon.

So scrupulously was the order of secrecy observed that it was not until many years afterward that anything definite was known of what took place in the convention. In the period following the War of 1812, when important questions involving constitutional interpretation were before the public, congress ordered to be printed all of the acts and proceedings of the convention that were in the possession of the government. The result was disappointing. The minutes of the secretary had not been well kept, and were never written out as they should have been into a complete journal. At best, they consisted only of formal motions and of the votes by states. But the seal of secrecy was broken and at various times from that day to this there have come to light the notes and records kept by different members. Most of these are fragmentary. There was one man, however, who recognized the importance of this gathering, and appreciated the interest that in all probability would attach to its proceedings, and who determined to leave as complete a record as was possible of all that took place. That man was Madison, and he set about his self-imposed task in his usual methodical way, that is best described in his own words: "I chose a seat in front of the presiding member, with the other members on my right and left hand. In this favorable position for hearing all that passed, I noted in terms legible and in abbreviations and marks intelligible to myself, what was read from the Chair or spoken by the members; and losing not a moment unnecessarily between the adjournment and reassembling of the Convention, I was enabled to write out my daily notes during the session, or within a few finishing days after its close." Madison later told Governor Edward Coles that the labor of writing out the debates, added to the confinement to which his attendance in convention subjected him, almost killed him, but that having undertaken the task, he was determined to accomplish it. He took his work so seriously that it seemed to have stifled any sense of humor he is said to have possessed and deprived his notes of any enlivening qualities. But every student of the subject is under the deepest obligation to him. From his Debates, as supplemented by the other very irregular notes, one is able to obtain a fairly accurate and complete account of the proceedings.

When taking up the all-important work of the convention in framing the constitution of the United States, it is well to keep certain facts and conditions continually in mind. In the first place, while there were fifty-five delegates who attended the convention at one time or another, that is not the number of those who were usually present. Some delegates were late in arriving in Philadelphia, some left early, and many were irregular in their attendance. From a careful study of all available data, supported by a single contemporary statement, it would seem that the average attendance was little if any more than thirty. Accordingly, as we use the terms at the present time, this body was more like a large committee than a convention.

In the next place, the importance of the occasion was recognized by the delegates as well as by the public generally. When they and their work were the subject of prayer and preaching in the churches, when they became the second toast at banquets, following directly after "The United States!", it is not surprising that the members of the convention took their work seriously, and that some of the delegates took themselves seriously, too. Madison asserted in the convention, and Hamilton repeated after him, that they "were now to decide for ever the fate of Republican Government." A few days later, Gouverneur Morris said that "the whole human race will be affected by the proceedings of this Convention." And after the convention was over Wilson said: "After the lapse of six thousand years since the creation of the world, America now presents the first instance of a people assembled to weigh deliberately and calmly, and to decide leisurely and peaceably, upon the form of government by which they will bind themselves and their posterity."[2] Of course those who were the most sincere in their desire and efforts for reform would be the most constant in their attendance. The convention accordingly was not merely a small gathering, it was also imbued with an unusually serious spirit.

In the third place, there is ample evidence to show that there was not a little social intercourse among the delegates, and it is inevitable that at such times there should have been considerable discussion of convention topics. At other times there were semi-formal gatherings, that might almost be termed caucuses, of particular parties or groups, where plans were formulated and agreements reached to support or oppose particular measures. It also happened that quite a number of the delegates were staying at the Indian Queen, a tavern on Fourth Street,

[2] McMaster and Stone, *Pennsylvania and the Federal Constitution*, p. 222.

between Market and Chestnut, among whom were Gorham, Strong, Hamilton, Madison, Mason, Rutledge, and Charles Pinckney; and the mere fact that they had a "Hall" where they lived by themselves is significant. To what extent outside meetings and discussions were held, or what part they took in the final results, will probably never be known. Their existence, however, should be recognized. Particularly in the matter of concessions and compromises extra-conventional conferences were doubtless of distinct service. Personal influence must have been an important factor in the work of the convention; and then, as now, it could be exerted more effectively outside than inside the formal sessions.

Finally, there is the paramount but evasive element to which reference has just been made, namely that of personal influence. Its greatest effect must have been felt outside of the formal sessions, but the extent of this can never be known. It must have been also a considerable element in the formal sessions of the convention, and even here it is a difficult factor with which to reckon. In describing the personality of the various members of the different state delegations an attempt was made to render somewhat at least of the contemporary viewpoint, that is to bring out the probable attitude of the delegates toward any particular member. From the fact that the votes were recorded by states it is generally lost sight of that the votes of individuals were apparently known, at least in many instances. Madison records the votes of particular individuals a number of different times, apparently to show the men in support or in opposition to questions of importance or in which he was particularly interested.

It is a difficult, if not a dangerous thing, to attempt to ascribe controlling importance or influence to any particular men where the evidence is so scanty. The parts which were taken by various men in the debates of the convention will be partially brought out in describing the proceedings, but it seems worth while to notice one man who took no part in the discussions but whose influence is believed to have been important. That man was George Washington, the presiding officer of the convention. His commanding presence and the respect amounting almost to awe which he inspired must have carried weight, especially in so small a gathering in the "long room" with the president sitting on a raised platform. In confirmation of this belief an amusing anecdote is told of an incident quite early in the proceedings. One of the members dropped a copy of the propositions which were before the convention for consideration, and it was picked up by another of the delegates and handed to General Washington. After the debates of the day were over, just before putting the question of adjournment, Washington arose from his seat and reprimanded the member for his carelessness. " 'I must entreat Gentlemen to be more careful, least our transactions get into the News Papers, and disturb the public repose by premature speculations. I know not whose Paper it is, but there it is (throwing it down on the table), let him who owns it take it.' At the same time he bowed, picked up his Hat, and quitted the room with a dignity so severe that every Person seemed alarmed. . . . It is something remarkable that no Person ever owned the Paper." Another anecdote is told, but not on so good authority, which indicates that Washington did not act with the impartiality which we ascribe to the ordinary presiding officer: that he allowed his sympathies to be shown; and that he actually beamed his approval and frowned his disapproval of sentiments that were offered. Whether or not this were the case, Washington's was evidently a name to conjure with and if Washington's opinions were known they must have carried weight.

And Washington's opinions were known. In the interval that elapsed while the delegates were gathering and the convention was organizing, there had been much informal discussion of the work to be done, of which this incident was related by Gouverneur Morris. It happened one morning in the convention hall, before a quorum had arrived, that some of those present advocated half measures as more likely to meet the approval of the people than any thoroughgoing reform. Washington interrupted the discussion with an expression of opinion that established his position beyond all question: "It is too probable that no plan we propose will be adopted. Perhaps another dreadful conflict is to be sustained. If to please the people, we offer what we ourselves disapprove, how can we afterwards defend our work? Let us raise a standard to which the wise and the honest can repair. The event is in the hand of God." Furthermore, in the convention itself, where tradition ascribes to Washington the rôle of the non-participating presiding officer, we know many of Washington's opinions. Luther Martin mentions the fact that Washington evidently approved of what was being done on certain occasions, and there are several references to him in the debates. But what is more important is that, in spite of his being in the chair, he voted with the delegates from Virginia, and Madison several times records Washington's individual vote to show that he was on Madison's side of the question. All of which indicate that it was apparently well known how Washington stood on almost every important matter before the convention.

Intangible as it may be, impossible as it is to estimate either its extent or its strength, the mere existence of the personal element should be recognized and kept in mind. Complications arose and solutions were found that are explicable only on the assumption of the influence of this indefinite factor.

CHAPTER V

THE VIRGINIA PLAN

Virginia had taken the lead in bringing about the convention and it was generally felt to be incumbent upon the deputation from that state to suggest a plan of action. Her delegates accordingly took advantage of the delay in forming a quorum to meet together for two or three hours every day, and they agreed upon a series of resolutions to be presented for the consideration of their fellow delegates. It was on May 29, as soon as the work of organization was completed, that Governor Randolph, on behalf of the Virginia delegation, presented this outline to the convention. Internal evidence shows much of Madison's handiwork in forming these resolutions, but from the fact that they were presented by Randolph they were commonly referred to as the Randolph Resolutions; they are more properly designated as the Virginia Plan. These resolutions are important, because amended and expanded they were developed step by step until they finally became the constitution of the United States.

In thus opening the main business, Randolph made an elaborate speech in which he enumerated several of the most glaring deficiencies in the existing government. He declared the confederation unequal to meeting the crisis and proposed as the basis of a remedy the fifteen resolutions which made up the Virginia plan. While the very first resolution stated that the articles of confederation ought to be "corrected and enlarged," the changes proposed were so radical that it was really a new instrument of government which was thus recommended. It was even said that Randolph "candidly confessed that they were not intended for a federal[1] government—he meant a strong *consolidated* union."

In the first place, provision was made for the separation of the three branches of government— legislative, executive, and judicial. In the second place the legislature was to consist of two houses, of which the first branch was to be elected by the people of the several states, the second branch was to be chosen by the first out of persons nominated by the state legislatures, and the voting in both branches was to be proportional either to the quotas of contribution or to the number of free inhabitants, or to both. This legislature was to have the legislative powers of the congress of the

---

[1] During the early part of the convention the term "federal" was used to refer to a confederation as distinguished from a national government. It was not until later that it received its present significance.

confederation, with additional powers to cover all cases where the separate states would be incompetent, together with the right to negative state laws infringing upon the "Articles of Union" and to use force against any state failing to fulfil its duty.

In the next place, the executive was to be chosen by the national legislature, and was to be ineligible for a second term. The executive and "a convenient number of the national judiciary" were to constitute a council of revision with a veto upon legislative acts that might, however, be overruled by a subsequent vote of both houses. Then there was to be a national judiciary, of a supreme and inferior courts, chosen by the legislature "to hold their offices during good behaviour," with jurisdiction in maritime questions, in cases where foreigners were interested, or which respected "the collection of the national revenue, impeachments of any national officers, and questions which may involve the national peace and harmony."

Provision was also to be made for the admission of new states by less than a unanimous vote, for the guarantee to each state of a republican government and of its territory, for the amendment of the articles of union without the consent of the national legislature, and for the binding of state officers by oath to support the articles of union. Finally it was proposed that whatever amendments might be prepared embodying these changes should be submitted, after their approval by congress, to conventions specially chosen for the purpose by the people of each state.

As some time at the opening of the session had been consumed in completing the details of organization, and as Randolph had made a "long and elaborate speech," by the time he had finished the hour of adjournment was approaching. The convention therefore decided that it would take the Virginia plan into consideration on the next day, and for that purpose it determined to resolve itself into a committee of the whole house, as that would permit of freer discussion and less formal action.

Another plan was then presented to the convention by Charles Pinckney of South Carolina. It seems that he had prepared this plan before coming to Philadelphia, and he evidently expected to deliver a speech in explanation of his ideas. Owing to the lateness of the hour, however, he could do nothing more than lay the document before the house. The effort of an individual would carry little weight in comparison with the proposals of an important delegation like Virginia's, and it is quite possible that the convention regarded this action by one of its youngest members as somewhat presumptuous.

At any rate, in what appears to have been a purely formal way, Pinckney's plan was referred to the committee of the whole and did not form a subject of discussion at any time.

On May 30, in accordance with the vote of the previous day, the convention resolved itself into a committee of the whole and Nathaniel Gorham of Massachusetts was placed in the chair. Daily thereafter until the thirteenth of June, the same procedure was followed. That is, for two weeks, except for purely formal business the convention continued in committee, and the only subject of discussion was the Virginia plan as embodied in the resolutions presented by Randolph.

The first of the resolutions was general or introductory in its nature and provided "that the Articles of Confederation ought to be so corrected and enlarged, as to accomplish the objects proposed by their institution." The objection being made that this was incompatible with the changes involved in the subsequent resolutions, Randolph proposed to substitute three resolutions, of which the first was "that a Union of the States merely federal will not accomplish the objects proposed by the Articles of Confederation." Again objection was made that since the convention was appointed to revise the confederation, to declare it incapable of amendment was to put an end to the meeting at once. Accordingly the third substitute resolution was taken up, "that a *national* government ought to be established consisting of a *supreme* Legislative, Executive and Judiciary." Although the discussion which followed turned "less on its general merits than on the force and extent of the particular terms *national & supreme,*" the questions raised were of the first importance, especially as to the powers of the convention to consider anything beyond amendments to the articles of confederation. The substitute resolution was finally adopted by a vote which was fairly indicative of subsequent lines of division: Massachusetts, Pennsylvania, Delaware, Virginia, North Carolina, and South Carolina were in the affirmative, Connecticut was in the negative, and New York's vote was divided, Hamilton being in favor and Yates opposed.

With the arrival of additional delegates from day to day the opponents to the Virginia plan were increased. Lansing of New York sided with Yates against Hamilton and cast the vote of that state accordingly. New Jersey and Maryland being represented were entitled to vote and were found in the opposition. Delaware also went over to the other side, which was partly accounted for by the instructions to its delegates, and partly by the fact that the combination had become strong enough to make opposition worth while. Of the new arrivals, the position of Georgia alone was uncertain and its delegates might be won over to either side.

It having been agreed to proceed upon lines of somewhat radical reform, the questions with regard to the nature and extent of the reorganization became important. As involving fundamental principles, the subject of the composition of the legislature quite naturally provoked the most discussion. That the legislature should consist of two houses was readily and unanimously accepted. Mason voiced the general opinion very well when he said a few days later that "the mind of the people of America . . . was unsettled as to some points: but . . . In two points he was sure it was well settled. 1. in an attachment to Republican Government. 2. in an attachment to more than one branch in the Legislature." There is a tradition that Thomas Jefferson some two years later, upon his return from France, was protesting to Washington against the establishment of two houses in the legislature. The incident occurred at the breakfast-table, and Washington asked: "Why did you pour that coffee into your saucer?" "To cool it," replied Jefferson. "Even so," said Washington, "we pour legislation into the senatorial saucer to cool it."

On the all-important question of proportional representation, the problem of the powers of the delegates, notably of Delaware, was again raised. But the convention proceeded with a fine disregard for that, and the real fight was made on the principle of proportional representation in the lower house. The leaders of the opposition in debate were Brearley and Paterson of New Jersey, and when it came to a vote on this question, the New Jersey delegation could only obtain the support of New York and Delaware, with Maryland divided. Seven states voted against them. That the representation should be proportional to population and that five slaves should be counted as three freemen was adopted with only New Jersey and Delaware in the negative. To apply the principle of proportional representation to the upper house as well called forth a stronger opposition. Maryland's vote was no longer divided, and Connecticut too was found in the negative. Still this was not enough to defeat the proposal, and the resolution was adopted by six states against five. The opposition had lost, but the minority was large enough and strong enough to encourage further efforts, and measures were concerted to forward their views.

The method of choosing the members of the legislature also caused considerable discussion. Sherman, Gerry, and the two Pinckneys were conspicuous in their support of election by the state legislatures, while Wilson, Madison, and Mason championed election by the people. Through a vote to reconsider, the question of the election of the lower house was twice the subject of debate, and twice the committee voted by large majorities in favor of an election by the people of the several states. For the election of the members of the upper house, the method proposed in the Virginia plan was unsatisfactory, that is, of an election by the lower house out of nominations made by the state legislatures. Where the idea originated of allowing the state legislatures directly to make the choice, it would be difficult to say. In one form or another it was suggested by several speakers at different times in the debate. And when for the second time it was decided that the lower house should be elected by the people, the sentiment in favor of electing the other house by the state legislatures was so strong that in spite of the opposition of Wilson and Madison it was passed unanimously.

The other questions regarding the composition of the legislature were of minor importance. The term of office for the lower house was fixed at three years and that for the upper house at seven. There was no specification for the lower house, but members of the upper house were to be at least thirty years of age. Members of both houses were to be paid out of the national treasury and were declared ineligible to state or national offices during their term of service and for one year thereafter.

When it came to the question of the powers to be vested in the legislature, there was a general willingness to grant extensive powers, provided they were carefully defined. The legislative rights of the congress of the confederation were accorded unanimously. In spite of the vagueness of the phrasing, the power to legislate in all cases to which the separate states were incompetent was granted by an overwhelming majority. The right to negative state laws contravening the articles of union was agreed to and laws in contravention of treaties were included, but the more general power to negative any state law was voted down. As doubts were expressed regarding the use of force against a state, the matter was postponed and apparently was never brought up again.

Another subject to provoke discussion was that of the executive. There were several of the delegates, conspicuous among whom was Randolph, who distrusted a single executive as savoring of monarchy, and who favored an executive body of three or more. But the convention decided in favor of a single person. Then the question of the method of election and of the term of office became important. At the very outset the difficulty arose that later developed into an almost hopeless complication. If the executive were to be chosen by the legislature, he must not be eligible for re-election lest he should court the favor of the legislature in order to secure for himself another term. Accordingly the single term of office should be long. But the possibility of re-election was regarded as the best incentive to faithful performance of duty, and if a short term and re-eligibility were accepted, the choice by the legislature was inadvisable. The only solution was an election by some other body than the legislature. Election by the people seems the most natural method to which to turn, but such a method was apparently regarded as visionary and impracticable. Wilson was the only one to speak strongly in favor of it, and he apologized for it as seeming to be a theoretical rather than a practical measure. The substitute he proposed was a system of electors chosen by popular vote in districts, but this was overwhelmingly defeated. In lieu of anything better the original proposal of the Virginia plan was adopted, that the executive should be chosen by the legislature. The term was then fixed at seven years and he was made ineligible to re-election.

Whatever may have been the intention of its sponsors, the result of the method proposed in the Virginia plan would have been to establish an executive who would have been the creature or the dependent of the legislature. But the convention had a decided preference for an independent executive and carried that idea out as far as it was possible at this stage of the proceedings. For instance, in addition to the usual executive powers and duties he was given the power of appointment in all cases not otherwise provided for, and in place of a council of revision the executive alone was given the right of veto, subject, however, to being overruled by a two-thirds vote of both houses. And what is perhaps the clearest indication of intention to make the office an important one is that the executive was rendered subject to impeachment.

That there should be a national judiciary was readily accepted by all. Nor was there any controversy over the jurisdiction of such courts as might be established; indeed, the clauses in the original resolution indicating the subjects of jurisdiction were unanimously struck out "in order to leave full room for their organization." There was also only a slight discussion over the appointment of the judges, which was finally settled by vesting the appointment in the upper house of the legislature. The most serious question was that of the inferior courts. The difficulty lay in the fact that they were regarded as an encroachment upon the rights of the individual states. It was claimed that the state courts were perfectly competent for the work required, and that it would be quite sufficient to grant an appeal from them to the national supreme court. The decision that was reached was characteristic of much of the later work; at this early stage of the proceedings, it might be regarded as prophetic of the ultimate outcome of the convention's labors. In other words, the matter was compromised: inferior courts were not required, but the national legislature was *permitted* to establish them.

The remaining provisions of the Virginia plan did not call forth much debate. The admission of new states by less than a unanimous vote was accepted. Instead of insuring to each state its territory and a republican government, "a republican constitution, and its existing laws" were guaranteed. The provision for future amendments was adopted, except that the clause rendering unnecessary the assent of the national legislature was dropped. There was a little discussion as to the propriety or desirability of referring the changes to be proposed by the convention to popularly chosen conventions in each state. Madison and Wilson favored it on fundamental grounds, King as a matter of expediency. Sherman and Gerry opposed it, the former considering the state legislatures competent, the

latter distrusting the people. Wilson and Pinckney suggested also ratification by less than the
whole number of states. The question of popular
ratification was once postponed, but the final
vote was in favor of it and it was so ordered.

The proceedings of the committee of the whole
had stretched over two weeks. In the course of
the debates there had been shown a remarkable
freedom of opinion. It was not to be expected
that there would be any sharp alignment of
parties at so early a stage of the work. Madison
and Wilson came forward prominently as the
leaders in advocating a strong national government. They were heartily supported by King
and Gouverneur Morris, and in general also by
Randolph, the Pinckneys, Mason, and Gerry. It
is a point not to be overlooked that Washington
and Franklin unmistakably cast their influence
on this side.[2] On the other side, were Sherman,
Paterson, Brearley, and Luther Martin, and
they were helped out by Bedford, Dickinson,
Butler, Ellsworth, Lansing, and Yates. As the

[2] Luther Martin, in his report to the Maryland legislature,
stated: "The honorable Mr. Washington was then on the floor, in
the same situation with the other members of the convention at
large, to oppose any system he thought injurious, or to propose
any alterations or amendments he thought beneficial. To these
propositions, so reported by the committee, no opposition was
given by that illustrious personage, or by the President of the
State of Pennsylvania. They both appeared cordially to approve
them, and to give them their hearty concurrence."

discussion proceeded, it became more and more evident that Connecticut, New York, New Jersey, Delaware, and Maryland were tending to vote together, in opposition to the other states led by Virginia, Pennsylvania, and Massachusetts.

It is apparent that this is nearly the same division which had manifested itself in the old congress, notably in connection with the adoption of the articles of confederation and the negotiations over the treaty of peace. It was a division between the states laying claim to western lands and the states having no such claims. It was a case of the small states against the large states, the former quite naturally fearing that they would lose their influence even if they were not actually absorbed by the latter. It has already been noticed that the question of proportional representation had stirred the small states most deeply, and that when they were outvoted, they were only aroused to further efforts. For the moment, however, it appeared as if the large states or national government party had won the day. On June 13, the committee of the whole reported back to the convention with approval the resolutions offered by Randolph as amended in the points that have been noted.

THE VIRGINIA PLAN

NOTE

THE PINCKNEY PLAN

In view of the misconceptions that are still current concerning the plan submitted to the convention by Charles Pinckney, it seems advisable to offer a brief explanation by way of warning. The document sent by Pinckney to John Quincy Adams, when the latter was preparing the journal of the federal convention for publication, and commonly printed as the Pinckney plan, was not a copy of the plan Pinckney submitted to the convention. No authentic copy of the original plan has ever been found. By critical methods it has been possible to determine the probable content of the original, and thus to identify two documents that have recently come to light. The one is an outline and the other a series of extracts from the Pinckney plan, which were evidently made by James Wilson in preparation for some special committee work. From these two documents it is possible to speak intelligently of what the Pinckney plan contained. These documents with further explanations may be found in the author's *Records of the Federal Convention.*

CHAPTER VI

THE NEW JERSEY PLAN

The representatives of the smaller states, particularly those of New Jersey, had been increas-
ingly dissatisfied with the way things were going.
The climax was reached when proportional representation was voted for the upper house as well
as for the lower. This action was taken on June
11, and it would seem as if it served to unite the
opposition. At any rate, when the convention
assembled on June 14, and was about to proceed
to the consideration of the report of the committee of the whole, that is of the amended Virginia
plan, Paterson requested an immediate adjournment to the next day. The reason given for this
request was that several of the deputations were
preparing a "purely federal" plan as distinguished from the one before the house and they
thought that they could have it ready by the
morrow. The request was at once granted.

On June 15, Paterson laid before the convention the plan which he and his supporters "wished
to be substituted in place of that proposed by Mr.
Randolph." The plan was frequently referred
to as the Paterson Resolutions, but Paterson was

only the spokesman of his own state delegation, which took the lead in this movement, so that the resolutions are more properly designated as the New Jersey Plan. But it should also be remembered that the representatives of Connecticut, New York, and Delaware, and at least Martin of Maryland, made common cause with the New Jersey delegates.

The plan thus presented was, as already intimated, in sharp contrast to the Virginia plan. It consisted of nine resolutions embodying important changes, but they were only amendments to the articles of confederation. In the first place, additional powers were to be vested in congress for raising a revenue by import duties, stamp taxes, and postal charges, and for regulating trade and commerce. In case the revenue thus obtained was insufficient, requisitions might be made upon the states in proportion to their population, counting three-fifths of the slaves, and collection might be enforced from delinquent states. The acts of congress and treaties were to "be the supreme law of the respective states," and the force of the union might be used against individuals or states to compel their obedience.

In the next place, there was to be an executive, presumably of several persons, elected by congress, with powers similar to those granted in the Virginia plan, except for the right of veto.

There was also to be a supreme tribunal, appointed by the executive, with original jurisdiction in cases of impeachment, and with appellate jurisdiction from state courts in maritime cases, in cases in which foreigners were interested, or which affected the construction of treaties or of acts for the regulation of trade or the collection of the federal revenue. The other changes proposed were relatively unimportant and did not enter into the subsequent debate.

After some discussion as to the best mode of procedure, so as to insure fair consideration for the new plan, it was agreed to follow the same course that had been adopted for the Virginia plan. It was accordingly referred to a committee of the whole house. In order that the two plans might be placed in due comparison, the amended Virginia plan was recommitted at the same time.

For the better part of three days the convention continued in committee of the whole. The debate was confined to a few of the leading men, notably Paterson, Lansing, and Ellsworth favoring the new plan, with Madison, Wilson, and Randolph opposing it. The speakers did not go into details, but contented themselves with contrasting the general principles of the two plans under consideration. The supporters of the New Jersey plan laid especial stress upon two points: that it accorded with the powers of the convention, and that it was more likely to be adopted by the country at large. Their opponents claimed that while they had power to conclude nothing, they had a right to propose anything, and they insisted upon the inherent superiority of their own plan.

In the course of this debate Hamilton delivered a speech to the preparation of which he had evidently devoted considerable care, and which proved to be the only important contribution he made to the discussions of the convention. He said that he had hitherto remained silent partly out of respect to the opinions of others, and partly because of the delicate situation in his own delegation, as he differed radically from the sentiments of his two colleagues. He felt, however, in the crisis that had been reached, that it was the duty of every man to contribute his best efforts. He accordingly expressed his disapproval of both plans before the house, but of that of New Jersey in particular. He declared his belief in the necessity of a strongly centralized government, and frankly said that in his opinion "the British government was the best in the world." He then read a sketch of a plan of government he had prepared, not with an idea of proposing it to the convention, but merely to present his own ideas in concrete form.

The chief differences between his plan and that

of Virginia were: that the executive and members of the senate were to be elected by electors chosen by the people, and were to serve during good behavior; that the executive was to have more extensive powers, including an absolute veto; and that the governors of the various states were to be appointed by the central government and were to have a negative upon the legislation of their respective states.

In later years, before the proceedings of the convention were made public, Hamilton had to defend himself against the charge of having favored a monarchy as the best form of government. The charge was based upon garbled reports of this speech, and was made for political purposes at a time when Hamilton was the most formidable opponent of the Democratic-Republican party. Hamilton had not proposed a monarchy. When some of his fellow delegates were hesitating through fear of public opinion, he expressed himself bravely and unequivocally for a strong centralized government that should be free from any danger of state interference. Moreover, he did not believe that a correct estimate of public opinion had been reached. He thought that the people were beginning "to be tired of an excess of democracy" and, he added, "What even is the Virginia plan, but pork still with a little change of the sauce?"

Hamilton's plan did not provoke discussion and it was not expected to. While the logic and consistency of his position were recognized, his ideas were too radical to meet with any general approval. As Johnson expressed it, the "gentleman from New York . . . has been praised by everybody, he has been supported by none."

It is altogether possible, if the New Jersey plan had been presented to the convention at the same time as the Virginia plan, that is on May 29, and if without discussion a choice had then been made between the two, that the former would have been selected. It would seem as if the New Jersey plan more nearly represented what most of the delegates supposed that they were sent to do. But in the course of the two weeks' discussions, many of the delegates had become accustomed to what might well have appeared to them at the outset as somewhat radical ideas. Then, too, the changes that had been made, insignificant as some of those changes were, rendered the Virginia plan much more acceptable. And so when the question was fairly presented to them on June 19 of a choice between the New Jersey plan and the Virginia plan as amended, seven states voted for the latter, New York, New Jersey, and Delaware voted for the former, and the vote of Maryland was divided. It is not without significance that this action was taken immediately after an able speech by Madison, the burden of whose plea was that the New Jersey plan would not "provide a Government that will remedy the evils felt by the states both in their united and individual capacities."

CHAPTER VII

THE GREAT COMPROMISE

The committee of the whole made its second report on June 19, again recommending the amended Virginia plan, and the convention proceeded at once to a more detailed consideration of the separate resolutions. The large-state men, having accomplished their main purpose, were now willing to make some concessions for the sake of harmony. For example, the objectionable word "national" was stricken out of the first resolution by unanimous vote, and it was "as of course" dropped out of each of the subsequent resolutions in turn. As some of the delegates were in favor of electing the members of the lower house annually, a compromise was reached between that and the term of three years previously established, and the final vote for two years was unanimous. Although the same unanimity was not obtainable, other modifications were made that rendered the plan less objectionable: the term of the members of the upper house was fixed at "six years, one third to go out biennially"; payment of the members of the legislature "out of the treasury of the United

States" was not insisted upon; and members of both houses were rendered eligible to state offices, though they were still declared ineligible to offices of the United States.

All of these matters, however, were of minor importance, and on the more essential questions the majority were unyielding. On the other hand, the small-state men had developed a more united and more determined opposition. This fact manifested itself unmistakably. In committee of the whole the vote in favor of two branches for the legislature had been unanimous, now the question found three states in opposition with a fourth divided. Previously Charles Pinckney had only been able to get three states to support his motion for the election of the members of the lower house by the state legislatures, now there were four states in favor of it with the vote of a fifth divided. Still the discussions were conducted with reasonable equanimity, though it was felt by all that the trial was yet to come. When the question of proportional representation had been under consideration in committee of the whole, Franklin observed that "till this point . . . came before us, our debates were carried on with great coolness and temper." And so it was now. For a few days everything went comparatively smoothly. But it was only the lull before the storm which every one could see approaching, and the suspense was hard to endure. If the storm could not be weathered, it was better to have the end come quickly. So on June 27, when Rutledge made the motion, the convention voted unanimously to proceed at once to the resolutions involving "the most fundamental points, the rules of suffrage in the two branches."

With the convention impatient to meet the issue, Luther Martin chose this most inopportune time, and in a spell of hot weather, too, to deliver a lengthy harangue. For more than three hours he continued and, having exhausted his own strength, to say nothing of the patience of his audience, he announced to the dismay of all that he would resume his discourse the next day. Some months later when they became engaged in a newspaper controversy over the adoption of the constitution, Ellsworth scathingly wrote to Martin: "You opened against them in a speech which held during two days, and which might have continued two months, but for those marks of fatigue and disgust you saw strongly expressed on whichever side of the house you turned your mortified eyes." Both Madison and Yates complained of the difficulty of following what Martin said, for he spoke "with much diffuseness and considerable vehemence." His main contention seems to have been that the general gov·

ernment ought to be formed for the states rather than for individuals, but his arguments would have been more effective if they had been more concisely and more opportunely presented.

Hamilton was greatly disappointed at the poor figure he was making in the convention. His ideas were too radical to meet with approval, and his vote counted for nothing because it was always overruled by his two colleagues. With all his keen interest in the outcome of the convention, he felt that he himself was wasting time. This feeling may have been strengthened by Martin's harangue, for Hamilton left the convention for New York the next day. He wrote to Washington, however, that he would return at any time if he could be of service, and he appeared in Philadelphia two or three times afterwards at irregular intervals.

When the convention finally got at the question of proportional representation, nearly three weeks were spent in reaching a conclusion. More than once any satisfactory solution of the difficulty seemed impossible, and the convention was on the point of breaking up. Gouverneur Morris afterwards said that "the fate of America was suspended by a hair." Feeling ran high at the very outset, and Franklin interposed with a motion that "prayers imploring the assistance of Heaven . . . be held in this Assembly every morning." It may seem surprising that such a praiseworthy proposal, especially considering the source from which it came, should meet with any opposition, but apprehension was expressed lest such a step at this late day might lead the public to suspect that there were dissensions in the convention. There is also a tradition that Hamilton opposed the motion on the ground that the convention was not in need of "foreign aid." The real cause of any difficulty in the matter was doubtless given by Williamson that "the convention had no funds." The incident threatened to become embarrassing when the question was avoided by adjournment.

On June 29, with Connecticut, New York, New Jersey, and Delaware in the negative, and with Maryland divided, the convention decided "that the rule of suffrage in the first branch ought not to be according to that established by the Articles of Confederation." Then came the question with regard to the upper house and it took the form of a motion to give each state an equal vote in that body. The delegates from Connecticut were responsible for presenting the question in that form, but it is doubtful whether very much credit or originality should be ascribed to them, as the idea had been frequently voiced in the previous discussions. The debate which followed was eager and eloquent. The Connecticut men supported their proposal with moderation but with great ability. Others on their side, such as Bedford and Dayton, were not so temperate. Wilson, Madison, and King spoke strongly, and sometimes bitterly, in opposition. Franklin, as usual, suggested a compromise. At an early stage of the debate, the New Jersey delegates proposed that the president should write to New Hampshire "that the business before the Convention is of such a nature as to require the immediate attendance of the Gentlemen appointed by that State." It was supposed that New Hampshire would side with the small states, so that the purpose of the motion was perfectly evident. But this was apparently regarded as rather sharp practice, and was promptly voted down.

Sunday intervened, and the first thing on Monday morning, July 2, the question was put on giving to each state an equal vote in the upper house. The vote was a tie, five states being in the affirmative, five in the negative, and one divided. This unexpected result was achieved through a combination of two circumstances: Jenifer of Maryland was absent, thus enabling Luther Martin to cast the vote of that state in the affirmative, and Abraham Baldwin, by changing his vote to the affirmative, divided the vote of Georgia. Luther Martin has stated his belief that Baldwin did not change his vote because of any change in his opinions, but because he was convinced that the small states would withdraw from the convention before they would yield on this point.   There is no other evidence to the contrary and all of the circumstances bear Martin out.   Although a small state so far as numbers of population were concerned, Georgia owned a great expanse of western territory and having been encouraged to look forward to becoming one of the large states her delegates in convention were usually found voting on that side.   In this instance, it was of importance that Baldwin was a former Connecticut man and so was doubtless in friendly understanding with the attitude of the delegates from that state.   Moreover, a temporary sacrifice of opinion for the sake of harmony was quite in keeping with his character. If his action forced a compromise, as seems probable, praise or blame is to be bestowed upon him according to one's point of view.

The convention was now at a standstill. After one or two suggestions were made that did not seem to meet with any particular approval, General Pinckney proposed a committee of one from each state to try and devise a compromise. Wilson and Madison strenuously opposed it, and though there were several others who did not think very much would come from it, the con-

vention generally approved and voted for the
proposal by a large majority. The members
were elected by ballot, and whether it was that
the small-state men worked together, or whether
the compromise spirit was so strong in the convention that it found expression in the selection
of the committee, it is impossible to tell, but it is
only necessary to read the names of the committee to see that the small-state men had won their
fight. The committee consisted of Gerry, Ellsworth, Yates, Paterson, Franklin, Bedford,
Martin, Mason, Davie, Rutledge, and Baldwin.
"That time might be given to the committee, and
to such as chose to attend to the celebration on the
anniversary of Independence, the Convention
adjourned till Thursday."

Little is known of what took place in the
committee. Yates recorded that the discussion
was largely a recapitulation of the arguments
advanced in convention and that as he himself
had not previously explained his position he took
this occasion to do so. He added that "these
remarks gave rise to a motion of Dr. Franklin,
which after some modification was agreed to, and
made the basis of the report of the committee."
Madison also noted that the report was founded
on a motion by Franklin, and further stated that
Sherman made a proposal which was not agreed
to "that each State should have an equal vote in

the 2d branch; provided that no decision therein should prevail unless the majority of States concurring should also comprize a majority of the inhabitants of the United States."

On July 5, the compromise committee presented its report, recommending two propositions "on condition that both shall be generally adopted." The substance of these proposals was: 1. That in the first branch each state should have one representative for every 40,000 inhabitants, counting three-fifths of the slaves, and that money-bills should originate in the first branch and should not be amended by the second branch. 2. That in the second branch each state should have an equal vote.

Immediately the debate broke forth again and recriminations were indulged in. Madison, for example, said that he was only restrained from expressing his opinion of the report through the respect he had for the members of the committee, and he intimated that he was willing to accept whatever consequences might follow its rejection. Gouverneur Morris was emphatic in his disapproval and was understood to say that the country must unite upon a reasonable and just basis, and that "if persuasion does not unite it, the sword will." Bedford apologized for the warmth of his earlier expressions that if the small states were driven to extremities they might find some foreign power to take them by the hand, but found some excuse in statements like that of Morris or like that of Gorham, who said that Delaware must be annexed to Pennsylvania, and New Jersey divided between Pennsylvania and New York. Williamson was ready to hear the report discussed but he thought the propositions contained in it the most objectionable of any he had yet heard.

The members from the small states generally favored the plan although some of them, such as Paterson, opposed it on the ground that it conceded too much. Still it was noticeable that the spirit of compromise was growing stronger. As it did not seem possible or, perhaps, advisable to vote upon the whole report at once, the different parts were taken up separately. The first part determining the ratio of representation was referred to a special committee of five for the purpose of fixing an absolute number of representatives from each state in the first instance and of providing for changes in the future. The other points, with surprisingly little discussion of the question of equal voting in the second branch, were ordered to stand as parts of the report, and the vote upon the whole was postponed until the special committee had made its report.

On July 9, the special committee recom-

mended: that the first house of representatives
should consist of fifty-six members, of which
number New Hampshire was to have two,
Massachusetts seven, etc.; and that the legislature should be authorized to regulate future
representation upon the principles of wealth and
number of inhabitants. The latter part of this
report was promptly passed without debate and
by a large majority, but the first part, specifying
the number of members from the various states,
was unsatisfactory, so that after a short discussion it was referred to a committee of a member
from each state. Then the house adjourned.

Promptly the next morning this committee of
eleven made its report, increasing the number of
representatives in the first legislature to sixty-
five. There may well have been some truth in
the charge that the numbers were "artfully les-
sened for the large States . . . in order to prevent the undue influence which the large States
will have in the government from being too
apparent," but the numbers assigned to the different states had doubtless been a matter of
compromise among the members of the committee, and several proposals in the convention to
vary these were defeated by large majorities.

The provision for future changes had been
vaguely expressed and Randolph now proposed
that, in order to ascertain the alterations in the

population and wealth of the several states, a census should be taken at regular intervals and representation arranged accordingly. Williamson suggested, and Randolph readily accepted the modification, that the census should be taken of the free white inhabitants and three-fifths "of those of other descriptions." A very brief debate followed upon the demand of the South Carolina and Georgia delegates that blacks should be counted equally with the whites, but a motion to that effect was voted down by seven states against three, Delaware only coming to the support of the two southern states. Objection was then made that the proposal was not in accordance with the resolution previously agreed to. That resolution had provided for future representation according to wealth and population, the present proposal left wealth out of account except in so far as slaves were property. Several voiced the opinion that the number of people was the best way of measuring wealth and that at any rate it was the only practicable rule of apportioning representation. The convention decided to proceed with the substitute of Randolph and Williamson but to divide the question. It was unanimously agreed that representation should be regulated according to the census. It was agreed by a vote of six states to four that a census of the "free inhabitants" should be taken, but to include "three fifths of the inhabitants of other description" was by a similar majority voted down. There was no sharp division here between slave and free states. On the first vote Delaware and Maryland joined with South Carolina and Georgia in the negative. In the second vote, to include three-fifths of the slaves, the states in favor of it were Connecticut, Virginia, North Carolina, and Georgia. There were evidently motives at work that are not observable on the surface, for the last vote apparently was not to the liking of the convention. Almost immediately afterwards the whole resolution, in the form in which it then stood, was rejected unanimously, and the convention found itself without having advanced a single step.

The discussion of this point had occupied the sessions of one day, July 11. The first thing on the morning of July 12, Gouverneur Morris proposed to add to the clause, empowering the legislature to vary the representation according to the principles of wealth and number of inhabitants, a proviso that taxation should be in proportion to representation. There was a brief discussion, the wording was modified to limit it to direct taxation, and it was then adopted by the convention unanimously. The main difficulty was thus solved and further details were quite easily agreed upon. It is worthy of note that Gouverneur Morris later wished to have this provision stricken out, although he himself had proposed it, because it did not accord with his own opinions and "he had only meant it as a bridge to assist us over a certain gulph." Before the day was over it had been decided that "representation ought to be proportioned according to direct Taxation and in order to ascertain the alteration . . . which may be required from time to time . . . that a Census be taken within six years . . . and once within the term of every Ten years afterwards of all the inhabitants of the United States in the manner and according to the ratio recommended by Congress in their resolution of April 18, 1783." The ratio recommended in 1783 was, of course, the three-fifths ratio. An amendment to have the blacks rated equally with the whites was voted down by eight states against two.

The convention seems now to have been in a better frame of mind. It may have had nothing to do with the outcome, but for over a week, that is, ever since the appointment of the compromise committee, the weather had been hot and on the night of the twelfth it turned cool. At any rate, the next two days were spent in discussing and modifying details of this and other features of the amended reports, and promptly on Monday morning, July 16, the whole compromise was adopted with Connecticut, New Jersey, Delaware, Maryland, and North Carolina voting for it, with Pennsylvania, Virginia, South Carolina, and Georgia against it, and Massachusetts divided. New York's vote was not included, as Yates and Lansing had left the convention a few days before, because of their dissatisfaction with the way things were tending and because of their belief that they were unwarranted in supporting action taken in excess of their instructions.

This is the great compromise of the convention and of the constitution. None other is to be placed quite in comparison with it. There have been many misunderstandings of it and many false interpretations placed upon it, but with the detailed sequence of events that has just been given it seems as if the main points should be clear. The important feature of the compromise was that in the upper house of the legislature each state should have an equal vote. The principle of proportional representation in the lower house was not a part of the compromise, although the details for carrying out that principle were involved. An absolute number of representatives from the several states was agreed upon in the formation of the first legislature, and the future apportionment was to be made by the legislature itself on the basis of numbers of population, counting three-fifths of the slaves, and direct taxation was to be in proportion to that representation. The proviso that money-bills should originate in the first branch and should not be amended in the second branch was regarded by some delegates as of great importance, but there were others who considered it of no importance at all.

The credit for the great compromise has been claimed by different men, and it has been ascribed to others. Of more recent years, through the weight of Bancroft's[1] influence, the credit has been very generally attributed to the Connecticut delegation, and the compromise has been quite commonly known as the "Connecticut compromise." It is true that the delegates from Connecticut were responsible for bringing forward the formal question. Introduced by Doctor Johnson, who spoke seldom but very much to the point and was therefore accorded a respectful hearing, the motion was made by Ellsworth "that in the second branch . . . each State shall have an equal vote." In the debate of the following day this was referred to at least once as the "Connecticut proposal" and once as the "Connecticut motion." It is undoubtedly true that the Connecticut delegates took an important part in getting the compromise adopted. But credit to the exclusion of others cannot be given

---

[1] *History of the Formation of the Constitution* (1881), vol. I, chap. 9.

to any individual, nor to any delegation, nor to any group of men other than to the small-state men in general. The combination of two methods of representation in one legislature was hinted at on May 30, the very first day that the Virginia plan was under discussion. On the day following, it was definitely and specifically suggested, and from then on it was frequently referred to until its final embodiment in the great compromise. With proportional popular representation established for one house, equal state representation for the other was inevitable, both from the ideas of representation that were current at the time and from the division of opinions in the convention.

The counting of three-fifths of the slaves, the so-called "three-fifths rule," has very generally been referred to as a compromise and as one of the important compromises of the convention. This is certainly not the case. Attention has already been called to the fact that this ratio was embodied by the congress of the confederation in the revenue amendment of 1783, that the committee of the whole by a vote of nine states to two had added it as an amendment to the Virginia plan, that it was embodied in the New Jersey plan, and that when it was incorporated in the great compromise it was described as "the ratio recommended by Congress in their resolution of

April 18, 1783." Indeed, one finds references in contemporary writings to the "Federal ratio", as if it were well understood what was meant by that term. A few months later, in the Massachusetts state convention, Rufus King very aptly said that "this rule . . . was adopted, because it was the language of all America." In reality the three-fifths rule was a mere incident in that part of the great compromise which declared that "representation ought to be proportioned according to direct Taxation."

In view of subsequent developments in this country, it is not surprising that historical writers have very generally over-emphasized the differing interests of north and south in the convention. A correct understanding of the situation, however, can only be obtained if it is realized that in the first stages of the discussion of proportional representation the conflicting interests of east and west were more important than those of slave and free states. In colonial times, as population increased and settlement extended into the back country, the conservative moneyed interests of the coast insisted upon retaining the control of government in their own hands and refused to grant to the interior counties the share in government to which their numbers of population entitled them. This was seen in its most obvious form in the inequality of representation in the legislature. Notably was this the case in Pennsylvania, Virginia, and the Carolinas. And this inequality was maintained in the state governments that were formed after the outbreak of the Revolution. In the federal convention, the same interests demanded similar restrictions. Pennsylvania's method of dealing with the frontier counties was cited with approval. As it had worked well there for the older portions of the state to keep the power in their own hands, so now in the United States, it was insisted, new states ought not to be admitted on an equal footing with the old states. Gouverneur Morris was the champion of the commercial and propertied interests, and when the great compromise was under discussion he declared in favor of considering property as well as the number of inhabitants in apportioning representatives. In explanation of his position he stated that he had in mind the "range of new States which would soon be formed in the west," and "he thought the rule of representation ought to be so fixed as to secure to the Atlantic States a prevalence in the National Councils." Morris was also chairman of the first committee of five appointed to determine the numbers of representatives from the existing states in the first instance and to provide for future apportionment. As a member of the committee, Gorham frankly explained that one of the objects in their report which the committee had had in view was to give to the Atlantic States the power of "dealing out the right of Representation in safe proportions to the Western States." This portion of the report was at first adopted, but was afterwards disregarded in the readjustment by which both representation and direct taxation were to be apportioned according to numbers of population.

In 1787, slavery was not the important question, it might be said that it was not the moral question that it later became. The proceedings of the federal convention did not become known until the slavery question had grown into the paramount issue of the day. Men naturally were eager to know what the framers of the constitution had said and done upon this all-absorbing topic. This led to an overemphasis of the slavery question in the convention that has persisted to the present day. As a matter of fact, there was comparatively little said on the subject in the convention. Madison was one of the very few men who seemed to appreciate the real division of interests in this country. It is significant that in the debate on proportional representation, he felt it necessary to warn the convention that it was not the size of the states but that "the great danger to our general government is the great southern and northern interests of the continent, being opposed to each other."

Again the ever-recurring interest in the question of the popular election of senators has led to misinterpretation of things that were said and done in the convention. In the proceedings of the committee of the whole, a momentary interest had been aroused over the election of the members of the upper house by the state legislatures. A good many years afterward, Madison went over his notes very carefully with the idea of their posthumous publication and at that point, in view of subsequent developments, he tried to make sure that there should be no misunderstanding by inserting the following explanation: "It will throw light on this discussion, to remark that an election by the State Legislatures involved a surrender of the principle insisted on by the large States and dreaded by the small ones, namely that of a proportional representation in the Senate." To make assurance doubly sure, when the subject came up again in the debate leading to the great compromise, Madison inserted another note: "It must be kept in view that the largest States particularly Pennsylvania and Virginia always considered the choice of the second Branch by the State Legislatures as opposed to a proportional Representation to which they were attached as a fundamental principle of just Government." It cannot be too strongly insisted that whatever opinions were expressed in debate, and whatever arguments were advanced for or against the election of the members of the upper house by the state legislatures—and all sorts of proposals of other methods were made and all sorts of opinions were expressed—they should be interpreted with reference to the one question at issue, that of proportional representation. It might also be noted that from the moment of the adoption of the great compromise the method of electing the members of the upper house was never questioned in the convention.

CHAPTER VIII

AFTER THE COMPROMISE

When the New Jersey plan was presented to the convention and Paterson had argued against the power of the convention to consider such a plan as that of Virginia, Pinckney had incisively remarked: "Give New Jersey an equal vote, and she will dismiss her scruples, and concur in the National system." This proved now to be true. The great compromise gave the small states an equal vote in only one branch of the legislature, but it was enough to reconcile them to the new plan, and they became warmer and warmer advocates of a strong national government. Not so with the large states, their plans were so disarranged by the loss of proportional representation in the upper house, that as soon as the compromise was adopted on July 16, they asked for an adjournment until the next day to give them an opportunity to consider what was best to be done. After a little show of feeling and some suggestions that it would be better to adjourn *sine die,* the request was agreed to.

On the next morning, Madison reports, before the regular convention hour, a number of the members from the large states met together for

consultation, and some members from the small
states were also present. It was evident at once
that opinions differed as to the consequences
involved in the adoption of the compromise.
Some regarded it as fatal to the establishment
of a strong government and favored extreme
measures, even to the point of recommending a
separate plan. Others seemed inclined to yield
and to favor a concurrence in whatever act might
be agreed upon by the convention as a body.
Apparently the latter view prevailed, and Madison adds that the smaller states were probably
satisfied "that they had nothing to apprehend
from a union of the larger in any plan whatever
against the equality of votes in the second
branch." The work was accordingly allowed to
proceed.

Many rumors were current as to what was
being done in the convention, and it is altogether
probable that something had leaked out concerning the serious differences of opinion that threatened to disrupt the assembly. If so, it was
important to allay all fears. Accordingly a day
or two after the compromise was adopted an item
appeared in one of the local papers. It was probably inspired and it was copied into several other
journals:

"So great is the unanimity, we hear, that prevails in
the Convention, upon all great federal subjects, that it

has been proposed to call the room in which they assemble—Unanimity Hall."

The next ten days were devoted to a consideration of the remaining resolutions of the Virginia plan. Quite the most important subject of discussion was that of the executive, especially with reference to the method of his election and to his term of office. Upon these questions the convention found itself in the same difficulties that had troubled the committee of the whole. If the executive were to be chosen by the legislature, he must not be eligible for re-election and his one term should therefore be a comparatively long term. But the possibility of re-election was a great incentive and if re-eligible, the executive's term of office should be short and he should not be chosen by the legislature. In this complication the delegates became hopelessly involved, and in the endeavor to extricate themselves every conceivable suggestion was made. Appointment by state executives, direct election by the people, and a system of electors who might be chosen by the people, by the state legislatures, or even from the national legislature by lot, were among the methods proposed.

Wilson noted with considerable satisfaction "that the idea was gaining ground, of an election mediately or immediately by the people." Among those who supported a popular election, direct or indirect, were Madison, Gouverneur Morris, King, Paterson, and Dickinson. Opposed to them were Randolph, Charles Pinckney, Sherman, Rutledge, Mason, Gerry, and Williamson. On a question for direct popular election taken early in the discussion only Pennsylvania voted "aye." The opinion of the convention on this subject seems to have been voiced in one respect by Mason when he said that "it would be as unnatural to refer the choice of a proper character for chief Magistrate to the people, as it would to refer a trial of colours to a blind man. The extent of the Country renders it impossible that the people can have the requisite capacity to judge of the respective pretensions of the Candidates." The other serious objection was that the people would always vote for a man of their own state, which would give the larger states an advantage over the smaller that would probably be decisive of the election. To obviate the latter objection it was suggested that each man should vote for two or three candidates, only one of whom should be of his own state. Another proposal was that the people of each state should name one man, and from the thirteen names thus selected, the national legislature should choose the executive. Both of these suggestions met with more or less approval, but for the time being they came to naught.

At one time the convention voted down a proposal for a system of electors to be chosen by the state legislatures, but two days later, on the suggestion that the number of electors in each state might be proportional, it was accepted. It was agreed that New Hampshire, Rhode Island, Delaware, and Georgia, should have one elector, Massachusetts, Pennsylvania, and Virginia each three, and the remaining states should each have two. After thinking it over for a few days, this plan was given up on the ground that to come together for the single purpose of electing a chief magistrate would be expensive and the best men in the distant states would not think it worth while to serve.

In a similar way every possible length of term was suggested. Four, six, seven, eight, eleven, and fifteen years were the more serious proposals. The last term, however, called forth a suggestion of twenty years as being "the medium life of princes." And yet "during good behavior" found its advocates, and four states actually voted in favor of a motion to that effect, rather with an idea of frightening "those attached to a dependence of the Executive on the Legislature" than from any preference for that tenure.

No wonder that Gerry should say that "We seem to be entirely at a loss," nor that Madison should add that "there are objections against every mode that has been, or perhaps can be proposed." And it is not so surprising that, after twice reconsidering the whole question, the convention should finally come back to the method in the report of the committee of the whole: an election by the national legislature, for the term of seven years, with ineligibility to re-election.

The other points relating to the executive were passed without debate, save in the matter of impeachment. King, Gouverneur Morris, and Charles Pinckney argued against it, unless the executive were to be appointed for life or were to be given too extensive powers. On the other side were Wilson, Madison, Mason, Gerry, Randolph, and Franklin. The latter arguments were so strong that Gouverneur Morris declared himself to be convinced and then made a strong plea for the necessity of impeachments. When the vote was taken only Massachusetts and South Carolina were in the negative.

In all these debates over the executive, while there was the greatest diversity of opinion, lines of division do not seem to have been clearly drawn. Members expressed simply their individual and personal points of view. Gouverneur Morris, for example, as we have seen, actually argued on both sides of one question. At the same time it is noticeable that the large-state men in general naturally favored a system which would insure to the large states a greater influence or a greater share in the election. This tended to bring them to the support of a popular election and to oppose an election by the legislature.

After the executive, the next most difficult subject was that of the judiciary, and here also the method of selection was now the chief point in dispute. Madison, Wilson, and Gorham strenuously opposed the method previously agreed upon, that is, of a choice by the second branch of the legislature. They proposed an appointment by the executive, and when that was defeated they moved for an appointment by the executive with the "advice and consent of the second branch." This was lost on a tie vote. Since obtaining equal representation in the upper house, the small states were more than ever in favor of retaining the appointment by that body, and they finally succeeded in doing so but only by the narrow margin of this tie vote. There was no difference of opinion as to the jurisdiction of the national courts, and the convention was content to declare in general terms that it should extend "to all cases arising under the national laws and to such other questions as may involve the national peace and harmony."

A proposal to unite the judiciary with the executive in the exercise of the veto power was again rejected and as before one of the chief arguments against it was that it would give the judiciary two opportunities to pass upon the constitutionality of a law. Closely connected with this subject was the question of the negative upon state laws vested in the national legislature. There was serious objection to any such power, especially as it was felt to be unnecessary, because the national judiciary would have the right to declare invalid such state laws as trespassed upon the fields of national legislation. The negative upon state laws was therefore taken away by a vote in which Massachusetts, Virginia, and North Carolina were the only states in its favor. It was Luther Martin who then proposed a modified form of one of the resolutions of the New Jersey plan which was unanimously accepted. The resolution as Martin proposed it and as it was first adopted was "that the legislative acts of the United States . . . shall be the supreme law of the respective States . . . and that the Judiciaries of the several States shall be bound thereby in their decisions, any thing in the respective laws of the individual States to the contrary notwithstanding." Contrary to Martin's intentions, that resolution with a single significant change developed into one of the all-important articles of the constitution strengthening the national government.

On the question of referring the new constitution to popularly elected conventions in each state, the sentiment in favor of it was much stronger than before. Randolph, Gorham, King, and Williamson argued for it more on the ground of expediency, while Madison, Gouverneur Morris, and Mason supported it as fundamental in the establishment of a new government. Madison "considered the difference between a system founded on the Legislatures only, and one founded on the people, to be the true difference between a *league* or *treaty,* and a *Constitution.*" Ellsworth, Gerry, and Paterson favored ratification by the state legislatures, but their motion to that effect only obtained three votes in its support, and the original proposal was then reaffirmed by an all but unanimous vote. Again the idea was suggested of the constitution being ratified by less than the whole number of states and of its being in force between the states so ratifying.

The only other item of interest in these proceedings was that relating to members of the upper house. When the great compromise was adopted, many of the delegates had supposed that the voting in that house would be by states, but since the main point of equality of representation had been gained, there was little objection to allowing the members to vote individually.

Three members from each state threatened to make the ultimate number of members in the second branch too large, and after it was decided in favor of two members, it was readily agreed that they should vote *per capita*, Maryland only being found in the negative.

The fifteen resolutions of the original Virginia plan had now been increased to twenty-three. With a few exceptions, chiefly in the provisions of the great compromise, these resolutions were of a general character and a working constitution must be a detailed instrument. It was perfectly evident that the convention itself could not prepare such a document without great loss of time and energy. From occasional references in debate, and from the fact that some of the delegates left Philadelphia several days earlier, it would seem that the method of procedure to be followed was generally understood. At all events, when the proper time arrived, without any hesitation it was agreed to refer the proceedings of the convention to a committee of five who should prepare and report a detailed constitution conformable thereto. The committee that was elected consisted of Rutledge of South Carolina, Randolph of Virginia, Gorham of Massachusetts, Ellsworth of Connecticut, and Wilson of Pennsylvania. On July 26 the convention adjourned and the committee was given until August 6 to prepare its report. Shortly before adjournment the committee was instructed to receive a clause requiring qualifications of property and citizenship in the executive, judiciary, and legislative officers. At the very last moment, in what appeared to be a purely formal way, the committee of the whole was discharged from acting on the propositions submitted by Charles Pinckney on May 29, and they were now referred to the committee of detail. Similar action was taken with regard to the resolutions presented by Paterson on June 15.

Four days before the adjournment was taken the delegates from New Hampshire arrived. It was too late for them to take any important part in the proceedings, but if we may judge from their private correspondence they approved of what had been done.

CHAPTER IX

THE COMMITTEE OF DETAIL

Rutledge, Randolph, Gorham, Ellsworth, and Wilson formed a strong combination. It was well that this was so, for the task before the committee of detail was not an easy one, and only ten days had been allowed in which to complete it. Inasmuch as its report was a definite and an important stage in the framing of the constitution, the significance of the work of the committee of detail is self-evident. Little has been written in the past, for little has been known of how the committee set about the preparation of its report. Within a very few years, however, certain documents have come to light which reveal some of the things that were done and permit a shrewd guess as to others.

It must remain more or less a matter of conjecture, but it seems probable that one of the first steps taken was to have some one of their number prepare a preliminary sketch of a constitution as a working basis upon which the committee could proceed. Doubtless this was done only after discussion by the whole committee, when certain general principles and ideas were determined. In view of the part he had taken, first in presenting and at various times in expounding the Virginia plan, Randolph was a very natural person to whom this duty should be assigned. At any rate, we have in Randolph's handwriting what is evidently the first draft of a constitution based specifically upon the resolutions the convention had adopted. Sometimes this draft goes into considerable detail, but at other times it only suggests what might be done, and it contains introductory and concluding explanations, with occasional running comments in the text. This draft was subjected to extensive and occasionally to radical changes, some of which were made in the writing of Randolph, but others were by the hand of Rutledge. The inference is that the draft was submitted to the committee, and after discussion and criticism, the modifications agreed upon were inserted by the chairman. As an indication that the document was one of a series, practically every item in it has been checked off with a pen.

It is quite possible that James Wilson had been working independently at the same time and in a similar way, but the next stage of which we have record shows documents in the handwriting of Wilson, presenting portions of the Randolph draft further developed, together with extracts carefully taken from the New Jersey plan and extracts from the plan of Charles Pinckney. These disjointed parts were then apparently worked over by Wilson and fitted together into a single harmonious document. This may have been done alone or with the assistance of the rest of the committee.

If it is realized that each of the processes which has been described in a few words represented no small amount of thought and labor, and that the ability of the whole committee had evidently been brought to bear at least upon the more difficult points, it will be appreciated that the Wilson compilation represented a fairly advanced stage of the committee's work. Certainly it seems to have been satisfactory to the other members, for it was gone over by them with the utmost care, not for the purpose of making important changes, but to see that the phrasing of the various clauses accorded with what they wished to convey. As in the case of the Randolph draft most of the changes made were in the handwriting of Rutledge, the chairman. This represented the last step in the preparation of the report, except that, as the document was to be printed, a fair copy was doubtless made before it was turned over to the printer.

The report of the committee of detail, as it was printed for the use of the members of the convention, covered seven folio pages with wide margins left for making notes. Upon examination it was found to consist of a preamble and twenty-three articles embodying divisions into forty-three sections and a still larger number of paragraphs. The first two articles were introductory, and the next seven articles, three-fifths of the whole document, were devoted to congress, its composition and powers. A single article, only a small fraction of the space given to congress, covered the executive, and another of equal length was sufficient for the judiciary. Two short articles placed certain prohibitions upon the states, and three provided for interstate privileges. The remaining seven articles were devoted to the admission of new states, the guarantee to each state of a republican government, the provision for future amendments, the taking of oaths to support the constitution, the ratification of the new instrument and the inauguration of the government under it.

In tracing the work of the committee through its various stages a number of interesting and important things are noticeable. The first of these is that the document which proved to be of the most service to the committee was the articles of confederation. It has already been pointed out that the new government in process of construction was radically different from the confederation, but that it arose from the attempt to remedy the defects of the old. That is significantly brought out here. The provisions for the powers of congress, the prohibitions placed upon state action, and the insurance of interstate privileges were taken directly from the articles of confederation, and sometimes word for word. A few important powers were added, but the significant change is the attempt to infuse into the new system sufficient energy and power to carry out the functions that had been granted to the old. With the qualification just stated, it is not too much to say that the articles of confederation were at the basis of the new constitution. In less important matters also, the articles of confederation were drawn upon, as in framing the introductory clauses, and in providing a method of procedure in settling disputes between the states.

In the second place, after the articles of confederation the next most useful documents were the New Jersey and Pinckney plans. These were used rather differently than the articles of confederation and more for the purpose of assistance in wording various sections and clauses. And finally, the state constitutions were continually drawn upon. Some of this was conscious, and some of it was unconscious borrowing. Just as in the convention the delegates were apt to propose measures with which they were familiar in their own states, so the committee drew upon their own experience, or in some cases copied specific clauses from a particular state constitution. The phraseology of the various state constitutions is so similar that it would be a wearisome and unprofitable task to attempt to determine the indebtedness of the committee to the different ones, but it is of interest that the New York constitution of 1777 seems to have been used more extensively than any other. In preparing his plan, Charles Pinckney had made extensive use of the articles of confederation and of the state constitutions, but of the constitution of New York in particular. Partly through the medium of his plan and partly through the document itself, the New York constitution was of great service, and especially in connection with the executive. Although the executive was to be called "The President of the United States" and was to be given the title of "His Excellency," the office was modelled on that of the state governors. In the specification of his powers and duties, and in the provision that in case of his death or removal he should be succeeded by the president of the senate, the committee followed closely the procedure in New York.

The importance of the legislature and its reorganization was indicated by the relative amount of space devoted to it. Yet a large part of this was given up to the specification of details, required by the general resolutions of the convention, and to the internal organization of the houses. The provisions for the latter were taken from the familiar procedure of the individual states and were of relatively little importance. Such were the provisions for deciding upon elections, for punishing members, and for choosing their presiding and other officers.

In general the committee made their work conform to the resolutions adopted by the convention, but room was left for the exercise of judgment, as in detailing the powers of congress and in defining the jurisdiction of the supreme court. In some instances also, it was inevitable that they should go beyond their instructions. It was found as impossible for the committee as it had been for the convention to agree upon qualifications for membership in the two houses of the legislature. Accordingly citizenship and residence only were inserted and property qualifications were left for the legislature itself to determine. In the same way, being unable to adopt a satisfactory uniform suffrage qualification, it was wisely left the same as might be provided in each state for the election of the popular branch of its legislature. The trial of impeachments was once more placed with the supreme court, but a practice with which the states were already familiar was adopted in granting to the house of representatives the sole power of impeachment and by limiting the judgment in case of conviction to removal from office and to future disqualification for office. In specifying the jurisdiction of the supreme court the committee took the liberty of inserting that all criminal trials should be by jury. In place of allowing congress to appoint ambassadors, to make treaties and to settle disputes between the states, as had been the case under the confederation, those functions were now transferred to the senate, the body which most nearly corresponded to the old congress as the representative of the states, and the disputes between states to be settled in this way were limited to those regarding territory or jurisdiction.

Thus far little is to be expressed beyond praise for the committee's work, but certain liberties were taken which demanded explanation. The convention had agreed that the president should be paid by the national government, it was understood that this would be done with the lower house and with the upper house the point had been left unsettled. The committee provided that the members of both houses should be paid by the state in which they were chosen, and from the clause on the payment of the president "out of the public treasury" was dropped. Under the provision for the admission of new states, although the resolutions did not warrant it, the committee stipulated that these states should "be admitted on the same terms with the original States." In guaranteeing protection to each state "against domestic violence," the committee limited this to cases where application was made by the state legislature. Further instances, the most conspicuous and the most important of all, were apparently due to the influence of the two southerners on the committee, Rutledge and Randolph: Provisions were added that there should be no interference with the slave trade, that no export tax should be laid, and that navigation acts should require a two-thirds vote of both houses.

The importance of the work of the committee of detail was generally appreciated, and it was a piece of work that was well done. Great credit was given to the members of the committee, and it is not surprising that they should take pride in it, nor that in later years it should be still more greatly magnified in their eyes. Ellsworth evidently had it in mind shortly after Washington's death, when his grandson quoted him to the effect that "Washington's influence while in the Convention was not very great, at least not much as to the forming of the present Constitution of the United States in 1787, which Judge Ellsworth said was drawn by himself and five others." For the present purpose, however, it is sufficient to regard the report of the committee as marking a distinct stage in the development of the constitution.

CHAPTER X

DETAILS AND COMPROMISES

It was on Monday, August 6, that the convention reassembled to receive the report of the committee of detail, and from then until September 10 that report was the subject of their deliberations. Every day for five weeks, and for five hours each day—and during one week for six hours each day—the work was kept up. From the opening day to the end of the month of August, William Samuel Johnson records in his diary only five cool days, and two of those were Sundays. Article by article, section by section, clause by clause, the draft of the constitution was discussed and passed upon. It was a trying and a wearisome task. Since the adoption of the great compromise and the protection of the interests of the small states in the senate, many of the opposition had been won over and were now working in harmony with those who were in favor of establishing a strong national government. It is little wonder, therefore, that before the end was reached many of the delegates became impatient with those who were stickling for points which to the majority seemed trivial and that toward the last, in order to bring the work to a conclusion, the large majority rode roughshod over the few in the minority.

If these points are borne in mind, and if it is remembered that much of the work during these weeks was purely formal, it is possible to pass rapidly over many of the things that consumed a good deal of time but that were after all of minor importance in considering the work as a whole. The spirit of compromise was clearly discernible in determining such details as the age and terms of office of members of the legislature. The qualifications of voters were settled in the same spirit, by adopting the report of the committee that they should be the same "as those of the electors in the several States, of the most numerous branch of their own legislatures." It being again impossible for the convention to agree upon any satisfactory rule of property qualifications for members of congress, it was decided to drop it altogether, and the committee's provision that the legislature might establish such qualifications was accordingly struck out. The question over allowing the members of congress to be appointed to offices that they themselves established was settled by prohibiting such appointment to any office which was created, or the emoluments of which had been increased, during the term of the members in question, and by providing that no person holding an office under the United States could be a member of congress.

The committee of detail had accepted the report of the first compromise committee and had placed future representation in the lower house "at the rate of one for every forty thousand" inhabitants. This ratio was objected to by Madison because the future increase of population would render the number of representatives excessive. Gorham did not think that the government would last long enough for that: "Can it be supposed that this vast Country including the Western territory will 150 years hence remain one nation?" By simply inserting the words "not exceeding," so that the clause read "not exceeding the rate of one for every forty thousand," the difficulty was removed and the section was unanimously accepted.

Annual meetings of the legislature were readily agreed to, but it was a question whether May or December was the better time of year for convening. Madison preferred May as the better season for travelling, while for December it was argued that a summer session would interfere with the business of the members, almost all of whom would probably be "more or less connected with agriculture." The latter idea prevailed, and the sessions were accordingly fixed for the "first Monday in December unless a different day shall be appointed by law." There seems to have been no intention, indeed no conception, that a long interval might elapse between the election of members of congress and their assumption of office. That unfortunate condition is the result of an accidental combination of circumstances attending the time of the ratification of the constitution and the inauguration of the new government.

The requirement of three years' citizenship for members of the house and of four years for the senate was regarded as insufficient in keeping foreigners out of the legislature. The time was accordingly lengthened to seven years for the lower house, and a proposal was made to increase it for the upper house to fourteen years. The question was a delicate one as several members of the convention were themselves of foreign birth. One of these, Butler, argued in favor of the restriction, frankly admitting that until he had lived in this country for some time he was not fitted to serve in public office. Wilson, on the other hand, spoke strongly against it. When he lived in Maryland, he had felt keenly his being barred from public office on that score, and besides it seemed anomalous to permit a man to share in the framing of a new constitution and then prevent him from holding office under it. Nine years' citizenship was finally agreed to as a suitable requirement for members of the upper house, although an unsuccessful effort was made by Wilson to have both this and the requirement for the lower house reduced in length.

One of the cases in which the committee of detail had exceeded its powers was in providing for the payment of the members of both houses of the legislature by the states in which they were chosen. When this clause came before the convention there was little discussion of the matter at all. By a large majority it was voted that they should be paid out of the national treasury. This was considered necessary to render them independent of the states. There was objection to fixing in the constitution the amount of the payment because of the changes that would take place in the value of money. To avoid the difficulty a previous suggestion of Madison's was considered that some other standard of value should be taken, such as wheat. This was not considered feasible, and it was finally decided to allow the legislature "to fix their own wages." There were objections to this method, but they were rather of sentiment or of delicacy, and it seemed to be the only practicable way.

The clause providing that money-bills should originate in the lower house and prohibiting the senate from amending them, which had been a part of the great compromise, was seriously objected to. This procedure was not copied directly from the British constitution but came through the medium of the colonial and state governments, where it had not proven an unqualified success. It was considered by some of the delegates as of no particular importance and it was opposed by others, on practical grounds, as being inherently objectionable. It was accordingly struck out, but the action caused so much dissatisfaction that the question was reconsidered. After a debate, in which several modifications were suggested and disapproved of and in which Randolph, Gerry, Mason, Franklin, Dickinson, and Williamson, argued in favor of the restriction, while Madison, Wilson, Rutledge, Gouverneur Morris, Charles Pinckney, and Ellsworth opposed it, the provision was again voted down. In recording the vote, Madison noted that Washington voted in favor of the measure, but he explained that Washington disapproved and had formerly voted against it and that he said "he gave up his judgment because it was not of very material weight with him and was made an essential point with others, who if disappointed, might be less cordial in other points of real weight."

The powers to be vested in congress were an all-important feature of the committee's report. The first stipulation of the convention under this head was that the new congress should have all the legislative rights of the old. And the surprising thing, especially to one accustomed to condemn the articles of confederation, is to see how large a part of the powers vested in congress were taken from the articles of confederation. The resolutions of the convention had further provided that there should be included in the powers of congress the right to legislate in all cases for the general interests of the union and where the states were separately incompetent, or where the harmony of the United States might be interrupted by the exercise of individual legislation. Under this provision the committee defined treason against the United States and provided for the punishment thereof; it provided for the establishment of a uniform rule of naturalization, for the punishment of offenses against the law of nations; and in two short clauses it granted power for the laying of taxes and for the regulation of commerce. A somewhat longer clause provided for the calling forth of the militia "to execute the laws of the Union, enforce treaties, suppress insurrections and repel invasions." And a very important clause was added "to make all laws that shall be necessary and proper for carrying into execution the foregoing powers, and all other powers vested, by this Constitution, in the government of the United States, or in any department or officer thereof."

The New Jersey plan had shown early in the convention that even the small states had been willing to increase considerably the powers of congress. Yet it is an indication of how far the members of the convention had progressed toward the idea of a strong national government that most of the extensive powers specified by the committee were readily accepted by the convention, and that most of them were, in fact, accorded unanimous consent. Some minor modifications were made such as "to declare war" instead of to make war, or "to provide and maintain a navy" instead of to build and equip fleets; a further power was added in authorizing congress to establish uniform laws on the subject of bankruptcy; and an interesting question was raised relating to the assumption of state debts by the national government.

Several members of the convention, among them Gerry, argued strongly for a positive injunction upon congress to assume the state obligations, as a matter both of justice and of public policy. The objections to assumption were based mainly upon the fear of benefiting speculators rather than legitimate creditors. The question was referred to a committee of a member from each state, and it was finally compromised by providing that all debts should be "as valid against the United States under this constitution as under the confederation." This left the matter in the same delightful uncertainty as before. Not long after this, Gerry announced his inability to accept the new constitution in the form which it had taken, and he soon became openly hostile to it. This hostility was charged to his failure to accomplish the assumption of state debts, for he was said to have speculated heavily in this class of securities. While this might have been in accord with the ethics of the time, in justice to Gerry it ought to be said that the charge was made anonymously in the controversy that later raged over the adoption of the constitution, and Gerry strenuously denied holding more than a very small amount of these securities.

A question was raised at this same time regarding the control of the state militia, and it was referred to the same committee that was considering the assumption of state debts. The reference of both matters to the same committee of a member from each state was probably made upon the principle that both involved questions of state rights. While the committee reported upon both questions at the same time, they were taken up separately by the convention. The question of the state militia was settled by granting to the federal government the right to pass laws securing uniformity in the organization, arming, and discipline of the militia, and the right to govern such parts of them as might be called into the service of the United States, while to the states was reserved the appointment of the officers and the training of the militia according to the discipline prescribed by congress.

Another question of interest and importance was with regard to the admission of new states. It will be remembered that Gouverneur Morris had favored the admission of new states into the union under such limitations as would leave the control of federal matters in the hands of the Atlantic states. Either on their own responsibility or because they interpreted the views of the convention that way, the committee of detail inserted a provision that new states should "be admitted on the same terms with the original states." When it came up for consideration Morris protested against this provision, and he made his objection on the same grounds as his previous opposition: "He did not wish to bind down the legislature to admit Western States on the terms here stated . . . [He] did not mean to discourage the growth of the western country. . . . He did not wish, however, to throw the power into their hands." Such men as Madison, Mason, and Sherman opposed him, but Morris succeeded in getting the objectionable clause stricken out, and then without a dissenting voice the convention agreed to his substitute: "New States may be admitted by the Legislature into the Union." This phraseology is apparently so artless that it might well obtain the unanimous support of the convention, but in view of its origin and authorship it acquires great significance. How great this is one hardly realizes until Morris's own interpretation of the clause is considered. Sixteen years later, at the time of the Louisiana Purchase, in a letter to Henry W. Livingston, he wrote:

"Your inquiry . . . is substantially whether the Congress can admit, as a new State, territory, which did not belong to the United States when the Constitution was made. In my opinion they can not.

"I always thought that, when we should acquire Canada and Louisiana it would be proper to govern them as provinces, and allow them no voice in our councils. In wording the third section of the fourth article, I went as far as circumstances would permit to establish the exclusion. Candor obliges me to add my belief, that, had it been more pointedly expressed, a strong opposition would have been made."[1]

[1] Mr. Justice Campbell, in delivering his concurring opinion in the Dred Scott case (19 Howard, 507), cited this letter of Morris's and it was also introduced in support of the government's cause when the Insular Cases were argued before the Supreme Court. It is interesting to note, however, that in the latter instance only so much of the letter was quoted as asserts the right to govern territory not originally belonging to the United States as provinces without voice in the federal councils. That part of

DETAILS AND COMPROMISES

The admission of new states naturally brought up the question of western land claims, and the same action was taken as in the case of the state debts. The matter was left *in statu quo:* "Nothing in this Constitution contained shall be so construed as to prejudice any claims either of the United States or of any particular state." This was attached to another clause giving congress power "to dispose of and make all needful rules and regulations respecting the territory or other property belonging to the United States."

On the other hand, it was felt necessary to place limitations upon the powers of congress in certain directions. A general restriction upon the activities of congress was to be found in the veto power of the president, which the convention had decided could be overruled by a two-thirds vote of both houses. In working out the details of this provision the committee seem to have copied directly from the constitution of Massachusetts, although Madison states it was modelled on

the letter which doubts the right of admitting such territory into the union was significantly omitted. *Brief in the Insular Cases,* Washington, 1901, 164.

Bancroft, *History of the Constitution* (sixth edition, II, 163), omits this particular letter, but cites others by the same hand in support of his surprising statement that Morris "gave his ancient fears to the winds," and proposed the clause in question "with the full understanding and intention that an ordinary act of legislation should be sufficient by a bare majority to introduce foreign territory as a state into the union."

New York. The convention accepted this with some minor modifications, and then changed the required vote to overrule from two-thirds to three-fourths.

The great compromise had provided that direct taxation should be proportioned to population, to which the committee of detail added that "no capitation tax shall be laid unless in proportion to the census." The committee of detail had taken from the articles of confederation the provision that the United States should not grant any title of nobility. The convention accepted both of these and added another provision from the articles of confederation: "No person holding any office of profit or trust under the United States, shall without the consent of the Legislature accept of any present, emolument, office, or title of any kind whatever, from any king, prince or foreign State."

One of the limitations placed upon the powers of congress by the committee of detail took the form of a statement of just what should constitute treason against the United States, and of a stipulation that no attainder of treason should work corruption of blood or forfeiture, except during the life of the person attainted. With some verbal modifications this provision was unanimously adopted by the convention, and a further provision was added that congress should pass no bill of attainder nor any *ex post facto* law.

While the powers of congress were under consideration, the convention approved the power "to borrow money," but disapproved the words "and emit bills," on the credit of the United States. Gouverneur Morris said that "the Monied interest will oppose the plan of Government, if paper emissions be not prohibited." Read "thought the words, if not struck out, would be as alarming as the mark of the Beast in Revelations." As it was generally felt that the government under the power to borrow money would have sufficient latitude in "the use of public notes as far as they could be safe and proper," the objectionable words were struck out.

British tradition had shown itself unmistakably in defining treason and in prohibiting bills of attainder, and another interesting manifestation of it came when the power "to raise armies" was under consideration. The convention first modified the wording of the clause so that it read "to raise and support armies" and then added the proviso that no appropriation should be for a longer term than two years.

The limitations thus far considered were theoretically important, but those placed upon the control of commerce were of direct practical concern. New England and the middle states were the commercial and shipping sections of the country. To require that all American products should be carried in American built and American manned vessels would have been a great stimulus to shipbuilding and commerce. But the south was a producing section. It had to have markets for its raw materials and it therefore needed free intercourse with the outside world. Such restrictions as had been laid on the colonies by the British government, before American independence, were greatly dreaded. Also, to meet its labor problem, the south needed an increasing number of slaves. The influence of the southern members in the work of the committee of detail has already been referred to in the provisions, that there should be no tax on exports nor on "such persons as the several States shall think proper to admit," and that navigation acts should require a two-thirds vote of both houses.

When these questions came before the convention, the prohibition of export taxes was objected to, but more strenuously by the middle states than by New England. Madison suggested as a betterment of the situation that export taxes might be laid by a two-thirds vote. This proposal was lost and Massachusetts then supported the provision of the printed draft. The prohibition of export taxes was accordingly adopted and by a vote of seven to four. The next clause of this same section, which was intended to forbid interference with the slave trade, precipitated a sharp although a brief discussion.

A few of the northern delegates and Mason of Virginia objected on moral grounds to the recognition of slavery in the constitution, and more particularly to the encouragement of that institution through permitting the slave trade. But the stronger resentment seems to have been against the attitude of the delegates from North Carolina, South Carolina, and Georgia, who declared that their states would never accept the new plan "unless their right to import slaves be untouched." To hold up the convention with such a threat was irritating, to say the least. There were others, perhaps a majority of the delegates, that were well represented by Ellsworth who argued in favor of letting "every state import what it pleases. The morality or wisdom of slavery are considerations belonging to the States themselves—What enriches a part enriches the whole, and the States are the best judges of their particular interest." It being doubtful whether a satisfactory settlement of the question could be made by the convention, a proposal was welcomed that the clause relating to the slave trade and the section on navigation acts should be referred to a committee of a member from each state. As Gouverneur Morris frankly expressed it: "These things may form a bargain among the Northern and Southern States."

The committee reported promptly in favor of no prohibition before 1800 of "the migration or importation of such persons as the several States now existing shall think proper to admit," but meanwhile permitting the taxation of persons thus imported at a rate not exceeding the average of import duties, and permitting navigation acts to be passed without requiring a two-thirds vote. After changing the date to 1808 and limiting the tax to $10 as the equivalent of the estimated 5 per cent import duty, objection was made to the vagueness of the terms used, and Gouverneur Morris proposed that the clause should read "importation of slaves into North Carolina, South Carolina and Georgia." This seemed inadvisable, and although attention was called to the fact that "as the clause now stands it implies that the Legislature may tax freemen imported," the convention accepted the first part of the report relating to the slave trade—New Jersey, Pennsylvania, Delaware, and Virginia being against it. The clause relating to navigation acts was postponed, but a few days later, an amendment requiring a two-thirds vote having been lost, the convention unanimously accepted this part of the compromise also.

This was one of the conspicuous and important compromises of the convention. It was not commonly so frankly spoken of as it was by General Pinckney. In the convention he argued against any restriction upon the passing of navigation acts because of the "liberal conduct" of the eastern states "towards the views of South Carolina." And a few months later in his state legislature, in answer to objections to the limitation of the slave trade to the year 1808, he explained: " 'Show some period,' said the members from the Eastern States, 'when it may be in our power to put a stop, if we please, to the importation of this weakness, and we will endeavor, for your convenience, to restrain the religious and political prejudices of our people on this subject.' . . . In short, considering all circumstances, we have made the best terms for the security of this species of property it was in our power to make. We would have made better if we could; but, on the whole, I do not think them bad." It is worth noting that the prohibition of export taxes was no part of the compromise. The point had been settled previously and was not referred to the committee nor was it included in their report. Undoubtedly the decision upon export taxes was partially responsible for bringing about the compromise in question, but it did not actually form a part of it.

As soon as the compromise had been finally adopted, a clause providing for the return of fugitive slaves was unanimously agreed to without debate.

When the compromise on the slave trade and navigation acts was before the convention, provisos were adopted that no "regulation of commerce or revenue" should "give preference to the ports of one state over those of another," and that "all duties, imposts, and excises, laid by the Legislature, shall be uniform throughout the United States." This action was taken as the result of an organized and determined effort on the part of the Maryland delegates. Dr. McHenry had been called home to Baltimore by the serious illness of his brother shortly after the convention first met, and he did not return to Philadelphia until the members reassembled in August to receive the report of the committee of detail. He then persuaded his fellow delegates from Maryland to meet together to discuss the report and to try and agree upon some common plan of action. Of several of these meetings McHenry kept some notes, and while there were different points with which they were not satisfied, they were especially concerned over the com-

mercial powers of congress. The modifications
noted above were among the results obtained.

Luther Martin reports another such gathering
of delegates: "There Mr. Gerry and Mr. Mason
did hold meetings, but with them also met the
Delegates from New Jersey and Connecticut, a
part of the Delegation from Delaware, an honorable member from South Carolina, one other
from Georgia, and myself." Of this latter
caucus we have no further record.

Sad experience under the articles of confederation had taught the United States the dangers
which lay in the interference with the work of
the general government through the action of the
individual states. An important feature of the
new government, accordingly, was the restrictions that were to be placed upon the states. The
committee of detail had prepared two articles on
this subject. The first prohibited the states
absolutely from coining money, granting letters
of marque and reprisal, entering into treaties or
alliances, and from granting titles of nobility.
The second prohibited the states, except with the
consent of congress, from emitting bills of credit,
making anything but specie legal tender, laying
duties, keeping troops or ships of war, making
agreements with other states, or from engaging
in war unless actually invaded. These sections
were important then, and they have proven to be

of importance since the constitution has been in operation, yet they were taken in the main from the articles of confederation. The provisions regarding the coining of money, bills of credit, legal tender, and laying of duties, were new and of great significance. But the greater significance comes from the fact that in the new instrument of government the limitation of the individual state's activity was more sharply defined and unequivocally expressed, and that it was to be enforced under a strong government. These restrictions were readily accepted by the convention. The prohibition of bills of credit, and of making anything but specie legal tender was made absolute, instead of permissible with the consent of congress, and the states were also prohibited from passing any bill of attainder or *ex post facto* law. A proposal by Rufus King, however, was defeated, that they should take from the Ordinance of 1787, passed by congress while the convention was in session, the prohibition of any law impairing the obligation of contracts.

To one who is especially interested in the judiciary, there is surprisingly little on the subject to be found in the records of the convention. We have already seen that the first question in this connection that aroused any particular discussion had to do with the establishment of inferior courts. The objection to these courts came from the feeling that cases ought to be tried in the state courts first and come to the federal courts only on appeal. When that difficulty was disposed of, by permitting but not requiring the establishment of inferior courts, a question came up over the method of appointment of the judges. The last determination of that question had been for an appointment by the senate, and for the present that was allowed to stand. The jurisdiction of the federal courts had not been determined by the convention beyond the acceptance of the general principle that it should include cases arising under the laws of the United States and cases involving the national peace and harmony. The specifications regarding this jurisdiction were thus left to the committee of detail. The committee having drafted this part of its report with considerable care, there was no objection raised except to the wording of a few clauses, the convention tending rather to an enlargement than to a limitation of jurisdiction. The cases under laws of the United States were extended "to all cases both in law and equity arising under this Constitution and the laws of the United States, and Treaties made . . . under their authority." All cases affecting ambassadors and other public ministers, and all cases of admiralty and maritime jurisdiction, were agreed to. Controversies between states and the citizens of different states seemed to include territorial disputes as well, and so the elaborate procedure copied from the articles of confederation for such cases was stricken out, and "controversies to which the United States shall be a party" was added.

That the jurisdiction of the supreme court should be original in cases affecting foreign ministers and in cases to which a state should be a party and appellate in all other cases, was accepted without question, except that the appellate jurisdiction was made to be "both as to law and fact." That the trial of criminal offenses should be by jury and should be held in the state where the crime was committed met with no objection. At this point it was also agreed that the writ of habeas corpus should not be suspended unless in cases of rebellion or invasion the public safety might require it.

Not a word in all this of that great power exercised by the federal courts to declare laws null and void if they are in contravention to the constitution. This power has been the subject of much dispute, and many have looked in vain in the proceedings of the convention for the authority to exercise any such power. The difficulty is easily solved. The question did not come up in connection with the discussion of the jurisdiction of the federal courts. At different times in the sessions of the convention, however, it was proposed to associate the federal judges with the executive in a council of revision or in the exercise of the veto power. At those times it was asserted over and over again, and by such men as Wilson, Madison, Gouverneur Morris, King, Gerry, Mason, and Luther Martin, that the federal judiciary would declare null and void laws that were inconsistent with the constitution. In other words, it was generally assumed by the leading men in the convention that this power existed. Perhaps Madison expressed this in the best form. He has already been quoted as saying that he "considered the difference between a system founded on the Legislatures only, and one founded on the people, to be the true difference between a *league* or *treaty,* and a *Constitution."* He then went on to say: "A law violating a treaty ratified by a pre-existing law, might be respected by the Judges as a law, though an unwise or perfidious one. A law violating a constitution established by the people themselves, would be considered by the Judges as null & void."

In three short articles the committee of detail had provided for interstate privileges such as extradition of criminals, recognition by one state of the legislative acts and judicial proceedings of another, and entitling the citizens of one state to the privileges and immunities of citizens in the other states. These provisions were taken from the articles of confederation, and with some modifications in wording were accepted by the convention without question.

The demand had been general that amendments to the new constitution should not require a vote of all the states, but the convention had gone no farther than to declare the desirability of amendment whenever it should seem necessary. The committee of detail proposed that on application of the legislatures of two-thirds of the states for an amendment congress should call a convention for that purpose. This was adopted unanimously.

The method of ratifying the new constitution was little discussed. There had been a general agreement previously that popularly chosen conventions were preferable to state legislatures, primarily because there was more probability that the constitution would be adopted by the former. The question then arose as to how many states must ratify in order to put the constitution into effect. A proposal for thirteen states was first defeated. A proposal for ten states was defeated by a small majority. Madison, Washington, and some others were in favor of ratification by seven states, and Madison proposed that the ratification should be by seven states provided they included a majority of the people. A proposal for nine states was finally accepted. It was risking too much to allow the new constitution to depend upon the approval of congress which might be fatally delayed. It was discourteous to ignore congress altogether, and so in a non-committal way it was finally agreed that the new constitution should be laid before congress with the recommendation that it be submitted to conventions in the different states.

These were the last articles in the report of the committee of detail, but that they were disposed of did not mean that the work was over. For one reason or another several articles had been postponed, and some of the most important points were still unsettled.

CHAPTER XI

THE ELECTION OF THE PRESIDENT

Whatever difficulties might have been encountered in other directions, they paled into insignificance in comparison with the problem before the convention of determining a satisfactory method of electing the executive. The previous troubles of the convention in this matter have been noticed, and it was observed that every solution reached was unsatisfactory. The difficulty now had become greater because the powers of the executive had been enlarged.

The resolutions of the convention had only declared that there should be a single executive with power to execute the national laws, to veto acts of the national legislature, and to appoint to offices in cases not otherwise provided for, and who should be removable by impeachment. In elaborating these resolutions, the committee of detail had made it the duty of the president to give information to congress, and had authorized him to recommend to that body whatever measures he thought necessary or desirable; he was empowered to convene congress on extraordinary occasions and, in case of disagreement between

THE ELECTION OF THE PRESIDENT

the two houses on the subject, to adjourn them.
He was to receive ambassadors, was to be commander-in-chief of the army and navy, and had
power to grant reprieves and pardons. In case
of death or removal from office, he was to be
succeeded by the president of the senate. As
already noticed the most of these provisions were
taken directly from the New York state constitution, and an interesting relic of that origin
was the authorization to "correspond with the
supreme Executives of the several states." From
an official designed to be, at the outset of the
convention, a dependent of the legislature, the
executive had developed into an independent
figure of importance. His functions might be
those of a governor, but they were of a governor
who was the head of thirteen states. No wonder
that some of the delegates stood aghast. Limitations had been placed in rendering the president subject to impeachment, and in making it
possible to overrule his veto of legislative acts
by a two-thirds or three-fourths vote of both
houses; but some further safeguard was necessary and the best was to be obtained in establishing a suitable term of office and a satisfactory
mode of election.

When an institution has been in reasonably
successful operation for nearly one hundred and
twenty-five years, it is hard to conceive the atti-

tude towards it of the men who lived before that institution existed. It was a new officer whom they were creating, and he loomed all the larger in their eyes that from the very limitations of their experience they were compelled to think of him in terms of monarchy, the only form of national executive power they knew. As an illustration of this take the account given by Baldwin a few weeks later to President Stiles, which was recorded by the latter in his diary: "As to a President, it appeared to be the Opinion of Convention, that he should be a Character respectable by the Nations as well as by the fœderal Empire. To this End that as much Power should be given him as could be consistently with guarding against all possibility of his ascending in a Tract of years or Ages to Despotism and absolute Monarchy:—of which all were cautious. Nor did it appear that any Members in Convention had the least Idea of insidiously laying the Foundation of a future Monarchy like the European or Asiatic Monarchies either antient or modern. But were unanimously guarded and firm against every Thing of this ultimate Tendency. Accordingly they meant to give considerable Weight as Supreme Executive, but fixt him dependent on the States at large, and at all times impeachable."

Another factor should be taken into consideration, namely, that these questions relating to the presidency were being considered with reference to the future and permanent policy of the country. It seems to have been generally accepted, it certainly was more than once referred to in the convention as a matter of course, that Washington would be the first president of the United States. In 1787 Washington was at the very height of his popularity and so great was the trust in him that no fear was felt regarding the inauguration of the new office. It is possible that the extent of power vested in the president was influenced by the same consideration. However that may have been, it should be borne in mind that this was a discussion of future policy, and it was against future dangers that the convention was guarding. Incidentally, it is indicative of the ideas of the time that, after the new government was installed, the title which Washington himself was said to have preferred as the most fitting one for his position was "His High Mightiness, the President of the United States and Protector of their Liberties."

The powers and duties of the president as defined by the committee of detail were accepted by the convention with some modifications that were mainly in wording, but an election by congress for seven years with a second term forbidden was no more satisfactory now than it had been before. After voting down by a large majority a proposal for an election by the people, and by a majority of one a proposal for an election by electors chosen by the people, the convention divided equally upon the general proposition for an election by electors. The further consideration of the question was then postponed. Shortly afterwards Wilson remarked: "This subject has greatly divided the House, and will also divide people out of doors. It is in truth the most difficult of all on which we have had to decide."

On the last day of August, the convention referred all parts of the constitution not yet finished to a committee of one from each state. The committee reported immediately upon some of the matters, and on September 4 reached that part of their work relating to the president. Although all of the ideas embodied in this report had been broached previously in the convention, the report came as a surprise.

The plan proposed for the election of the executive was a system of electors chosen in each state as its legislature might direct. The electors were to be equal in number to the state's representation in congress, that is, both senators and representatives. The electors in each state were to meet and to vote for two persons, one of whom should not be an inhabitant of that state. These votes were to be listed, certified, sealed, and sent to the senate of the United States. They were to be opened and counted in the senate, and the person having the greatest number of votes was to be president, *provided such number was a majority of all the electors.* In case of a tie, the senate was to choose immediately between them, and if no one had a majority, the senate was to choose the president from the five highest on the list. The person having the next greatest number of votes was to be vice-president and in case of a tie the senate was to choose one of them.

As qualifications for the presidency it was provided that the incumbent should be thirty-five years of age, a natural born citizen of the United States or a citizen at the time of the adoption of the constitution, and a resident within the United States for fourteen years. The vice-president was to be *ex officio* president of the senate but with a right to vote only in case of a tie.

Apparently on the assumption that a satisfactory method of electing the president had been discovered, the committee further recommended that the president now be given power, with the advice and consent of the senate, to make treaties, and to nominate and appoint ambassadors and judges of the supreme court, but no treaty was to be made without the consent of two-thirds of the members present.

As the matter of a council for the president had never been satisfactorily settled, the committee now recommended that the president be empowered to require the opinion in writing of the principal officer of each of the executive departments. No such departments were provided for in the constitution, but it was assumed that they would be established and that there would be a single officer at the head of each. Almost as if it were incidental, the committee also recommended that the president's and all other cases of impeachment should be tried by the senate instead of the supreme court.

The central feature of this report was the proposed method of electing the president, and that proposal was a compromise. The compromise does not appear on the surface, but it was referred to in the course of the debates, and in later years it was thus explained by several members of the convention, so that no doubt attaches to it.

The objections to a popular election, direct or indirect, were a lack of confidence in the knowledge and judgment of the people and a fear that any such method would give too great an advantage to the large states. Under the proposed system, as the number of electors from each state was to equal the number of its senators and representatives, the large states, with their greater representation in congress, would have a distinct advantage. To offset this, when no choice by the electors resulted, the senate was to elect the president from the highest five candidates on the list, and in the senate it was conceded the small states would have an advantage.

This was no pretense, a mere sop thrown out to the small states. It was expected that the electors would naturally vote for men from their own state, hence the provision that each elector should vote for two persons, one of whom should not be a resident of the state with himself. And each elector was expected to vote independently according to his own best judgment. Under those circumstances, it was conceded that Washington would be chosen in the first election, but in subsequent elections it was expected that the vote would be so scattered as not to give a majority to any one person. This would throw the election into the senate. In other words, and it was so explained again and again, and by such men as Madison, Sherman, King, and Gouverneur Morris, under this system the large states would nominate the candidates and the eventual election would be controlled by the small states.

The convention acted on the assumption that this would happen in the great majority of cases. "Nineteen times in twenty," Mason asserted in the federal convention, and a little later in the

Virginia state convention he claimed forty-nine times out of fifty, the vote of the electors would not be decisive. Several members of the convention thought that this "would not be the case," but after Mason insisted that "Those who think there is no danger of there not being a majority for the same person in the first instance ought to give up the point to those who think otherwise," it was tacitly conceded. It is quite possible that here, as in so many other questions, the large states accomplished their purpose under a veil of concession. It was not for them to dispute the improbability of an election resulting in the first instance. If they had the advantage in the choosing of electors, it was certainly still more to their benefit if, contrary to expectations, the electors were to determine the result.

The chief objection to the proposed plan of election was the additional power that it would place in the senate already vested with excessive powers. Several proposals to allow a plurality of electoral votes to determine the choice were voted down. In order to better the situation, it was agreed that two-thirds of the senate must be present at the election. Some one proposing that the voting should be by states immediately suggested substituting the house of representatives for the senate but retaining the principle of voting by states. Without any hesitation the convention adopted the substitute, Delaware only voting in the negative, and with a few minor changes the new plan of electing the president was acceptable to the convention. The committee had reported on September fourth and by the sixth the report was virtually adopted, although the final votes and a few minor points went over until the next day. Three days were, at the last, sufficient to settle this most difficult question which had bothered the convention for three months.

Serious objection was taken to the vice-presidency, and it was frankly admitted by Williamson, a member of the committee, that the officer "was not wanted. He was introduced only for the sake of a valuable mode of election which required two to be chosen at the same time." Then objection was made to his being forced upon the senate as its presiding officer. The convention, however, accepted the committee's point of view and voted by a large majority that the vice-president should be *ex officio* president of the senate. When the ultimate election of the president was transferred to the house of representatives, the provision for the vice-president was left as before, that is, the senate was to make the choice in case of a tie.

The avowed purpose of the new method of election was to render the executive independent of the legislature and thus do away with the intrigue and corruption inevitable to the other arrangement. In the previous proposals for choosing the president by electors, it had been the prevalent idea that the electors should meet together in one place. It was felt to be rather an expensive proceeding to bring so many persons from the distant states for the single purpose of electing a president, and such a meeting was thought to offer a splendid field for corruption. The new plan, accordingly, provided that the electors should meet in their respective states. Voting at the same time and at so great distance from one another "the great evil of cabal was avoided." A similar precaution was taken in the provision that when the votes were opened in the presence of congress, if it was found that no one had a majority "then the House of Representatives shall *immediately* chuse by Ballot one of them for President." Another safeguard was added by the convention in declaring that no person should be appointed an elector who was a member of congress or held any office of profit or trust under the United States. Just what was included under that dreaded word "cabal" it would be difficult to say. Besides intrigue and corruption there may have been a vague idea of political parties, but certainly there was no conception of the party organization that was to twist to its own devices the carefully devised scheme of the convention.

In view of the ever-recurring interest in the presidential term of office, it may not be amiss to state that the convention never considered the question of a "third term." Their difficulty was whether or not the president should be elected by the legislature. In the one case he should have but one term, and in the other he should be eligible to re-election. Six or seven years seemed to be the acceptable length of a single term, and four years was regarded as a convenient time if re-election was permissible. That is practically the only form in which those questions came up.

It was evident that the convention was growing tired. The committee had recommended that the power of appointment and the making of treaties be taken from the senate and vested in the president "by and with the advice and consent of the senate." With surprising unanimity and surprisingly little debate, these important changes were agreed to. The requirement of the concurrence of two-thirds of the senate in treaties was amended at Madison's suggestion to except treaties of peace. It was then adopted and the next day reconsidered and re-adopted after striking out the exception of treaties of peace. A proposal of a council for the president was rejected, although it was supported by Madison, Wilson, Franklin, Mason, and Dickinson. The convention then unanimously accepted the committee's recommendation "authorizing the President to call for the opinions of the Heads of Departments in writing." After very slight modifications, the trial of impeachments was vested in the senate.

As a part of the compromise in determining the method of electing the president, it had been agreed in the committee that the originating of money-bills should once more be restricted to the house of representatives. Gouverneur Morris and King referred in the convention to this feature of the compromise, and Madison, who was also a member of the committee, was perfectly frank as to the way in which this provision was used: "Col: Mason Mr. Gerry and other members from large States set great value on this privilege of originating money bills. Of this the members from the small States, with some from the large States who wished a high mounted Government, endeavored to avail themselves, by making that privilege, the price of arrangements in the constitution favorable to the small States, and to the elevation of the Government." The committee accordingly reported such a clause, but with the proviso that the senate might amend. When it was presented to the convention, it was deliberately held up, on the suggestion of Gouverneur Morris, to make sure that the other points were first adopted. When that was successfully accomplished, the convention accepted the clause. It had served its purpose as a compromise factor, and all virtue being taken from it by granting to the senate an unrestricted privilege of amendment, it was finally allowed a place in the constitution.

During the sessions of the convention, but it would seem especially during the latter part of August, while the subject of the presidency was causing so much disquiet, persistent rumors were current outside that the establishment of a monarchy was under consideration. The common form of the rumor was that the Bishop of Osnaburgh, the second son of George III, was to be invited to become King of the United States. It evidently seemed desirable to the convention to stop these rumors, for what was clearly an inspired statement appeared about the same time in various private letters and finally in the newspapers: "tho' we cannot, affirmatively, tell you what we are doing, we can, negatively, tell you what we are not doing—we never once thought of a king."[1]

[1] In the *Independent Gazetteer* of August 18, 1787, is this anecdote: "On taking down the CROWN of Christ Church steeple, which some time since had been much injured by lightning, one of the bystanders asked what they were going to do with it. He was told it was to be repaired and put up immediately. 'I guess,' says an

And yet one wonders if there were not some thought of monarchy.[2] The records show frank expressions by certain of the members that they considered a limited monarchy the best form of government. When McHenry returned to the convention on August 6, he reports that he saw his colleague Mercer making out a list of members in attendance with "for" or "against" marked opposite almost every name. On being asked what that meant, Mercer laughingly replied that those marked with a "for" were for a king. McHenry copied the list, and on learning what it was Luther Martin copied it likewise. There were said to be over twenty names favoring a royal government. Mercer later claimed that he said these delegates were in favor of a national government, but his statement is not very convincing and leads one to think that McHenry reported the incident in substance correctly. If some of the delegates were in favor of a monarchical government it is

arch boy, who had been very attentive to the query and answer, 'they had better wait till the Convention breaks up, and know first what they recommend!'" W. P. Hazard, *Annals of Philadelphia*. Revised from "Watson's Annals," Philadelphia, 1879, vol. III, p. 197.

[2] Richard Krauel in the *American Historical Review*, XVII, 44-51, presents interesting evidence to show that Nathaniel Gorham in the latter part of 1786 actually wrote to Prince Henry of Prussia with regard to the possibility of his becoming the monarch of the United States.

possible that, when the presidency was so much in doubt, they may have been circulating rumors of establishing a monarchy in order to try out public opinion. If so, the presidential compromise put an end to all such schemes at once, for of all things done in the convention the members seemed to have been prouder of that than of any other, and they seemed to regard it as having solved the problem for any country of how to choose a chief magistrate.

CHAPTER XII

FINISHING THE WORK

At the same time that the committee on the unfinished parts of the constitution presented its report on the election of the president, it recommended a modification in the first clause of the section detailing the powers of congress that has been the subject of discussion from that day to this. The clause as reported by the committee of detail read: "The Legislature of the United States shall have the power to lay and collect taxes, duties, imposts and excises." The modification now proposed was to add the words "to pay the debts and provide for the common defence and general welfare." The change was at once accepted by the convention unanimously and apparently without discussion. The question concerning it is whether it was intended to enlarge the powers of congress or to be merely explanatory of the preceding clause.

Two weeks before, when the assumption of state debts was under consideration, one of the forms of wording proposed was "to discharge the debts of the United States and of the several states incurred during the late war for the common defence and general welfare." At the same

time the committee of detail in a supplementary
report recommended adding to the first clause of
the powers of congress the explanatory statement "for payment of the debts and necessary
expenses of the United States." These two proposals were apparently merged in a clause that
"The Legislature shall fulfil the engagements
and discharge the debts of the United States,"
which was prefixed to the power of taxation.
Shortly afterwards this action was reconsidered
and the clause dropped in the non-committal
compromise: "all debts . . . shall be as valid
against the United States under this constitution
as under the confederation."

When this action was taken Sherman "thought
it necessary to connect with the clause for laying
taxes, duties &c. an express provision for the
object of the old debts and moved to add 'for
the payment of said debts and for the defraying
the expenses that shall be incurred for the common defence and general welfare.' " Madison
notes that the proposal was considered unnecessary and that only Connecticut voted in favor of
it.

Sherman was a member of the committee on
the unfinished parts of the constitution, and it is
noticeable that favored ideas of the individual
members were apt to be recommended by the
committee. Gouverneur Morris was also a

member and as a representative of the moneyed interests he naturally had been strongly in favor of a specific obligation to assume the old debts. These men probably had to do with the phrasing of the clause first referred to and with its recommendation by the committee. But whatever interpretation attaches to it, the wording and punctuation as originally reported and adopted are unmistakable: "The Legislature shall have power to lay and collect taxes, duties, imposts and excises, to pay the debts and provide for the common defence and general welfare of the United States."

Two days after this action was taken, McHenry spoke to several members regarding the inclusion of a power "enabling the legislature to erect piers for protection of shipping in winter and to preserve the navigation of harbours." Gouverneur Morris was one of those consulted and while he was in favor of it, he thought it might be done under the common defence and general welfare clause. McHenry was evidently surprised and somewhat wonderingly notes: "If this comprehends such a power, it goes to authorize the legislature to grant exclusive privileges to trading companies, etc." All of which is interesting and probably important as an indication of what Morris would have liked to have this clause mean.

While the convention was still engaged in the discussion of the presidential compromise, the committee on unfinished parts of the constitution also recommended a clause giving exclusive power to congress over the district for the seat of government, and another clause authorizing copyrights and patents. Both of these were unanimously agreed to.

By Saturday, the 8th of September, the questions regarding the executive having been settled, the work of going through the draft of the committee of detail was practically completed. Accordingly a committee of five was appointed "to revise the style of and arrange the articles which had been agreed to by the house." The committee was made up exclusively of friends of the new constitution, Doctor Johnson, Alexander Hamilton, Gouverneur Morris, James Madison, and Rufus King. On Monday, the 10th, a brief session seems to have been held to permit the discussion of a few points that were still unsatisfactory, and the convention then adjourned to await the report of the committee.

The only important action taken on Monday related to future amendments of the constitution. The provision in the draft reported by the committee of detail—that on the application of the legislatures of two-thirds of the states, congress should call a convention for that purpose—had been unanimously adopted by the convention. Gerry now asked and obtained consent to have this reconsidered, because he thought two-thirds of the states could thus commit the whole union to dangerous innovations. This move was taken advantage of by those who desired an easier method of amendment, to render it possible for congress to inaugurate amendments whenever two-thirds of both houses should think it necessary. Gerry evidently wished to require the consent of all the states to adopt an amendment, but Wilson proposed to require the approval of only two-thirds. When the latter motion was defeated by a majority of one, Wilson immediately suggested three-fourths and the convention adopted it unanimously. The proviso was then added, at the insistence of the extreme southern states, that no amendments should be made prior to 1808 that would interfere with the slave trade.

Gerry next moved to amend another section previously agreed to, so that the approval of congress would be essential to the adoption of the new plan. Though supported by Hamilton and others, the amendment was defeated. Randolph having previously expressed his doubts concerning the new plan now came out flatly against it. He wanted the new constitution to be transmitted through the medium of congress and state legislatures to state conventions. Then another general convention was to be held with full power to adopt or reject such amendments as might be proposed by the various state conventions. His motion embodying these proposals was laid on the table and the convention adjourned after instructing the committee of style to prepare an address to accompany the constitution.

By Wednesday, the committee of style was ready to make its report, which was at once ordered printed for the convenience of the delegates. The work done in preparing that report is probably to be credited to Gouverneur Morris. Shortly after the convention was over, Baldwin was visiting his former home in Connecticut and called on President Stiles. To him Baldwin stated that the work of this committee was done by Morris and Wilson. Twenty-seven years later, Morris wrote to Timothy Pickering that the constitution "was written by the fingers, which write this letter." And Madison confirms this in a letter he wrote shortly before his death to Jared Sparks: "The *finish* . . . fairly belongs to the pen of Mr. Morris. . . . A better choice could not have been made, as the performance of the task proved. It is true that the state of the materials . . . was a good preparation . . . but there was sufficient room for the talents and taste stamped by the author on the face of it."

A careful comparison of the draft reported by

the committee of style with the proceedings of the convention would lead one to think that no undue liberties had been taken, and yet just a little suspicion attaches to the work of Morris in preparing this last draft of the constitution. It is partly due to intimations that he himself gave, as in the case already referred to with regard to the admission of new states, when he wrote: "In wording the third section of the fourth article, I went as far as circumstances would permit to establish the exclusion. Candor obliges me to add my belief, that, had it been more pointedly expressed, a strong opposition would have been made." It is also due to stories that were whispered about in the years following the adoption of the new constitution. One illustration of that is to be found in connection with the "general welfare" clause just considered. In the report of the committee of style, this clause was separated from the preceding and following clauses by semicolons, thus making it an independent power of congress. That was not the way in which it had been adopted by the convention, but it was more in accordance with Morris's ideas. The change may or may not have been intentional, but Albert Gallatin a few years later stated openly in congress that "he was well informed" that this modification was a "trick" devised by "one of the members who represented

the State of Pennsylvania." In the constitution
as it was finally engrossed the clause was changed
back to its original form, and the credit for this
Gallatin gave to Sherman.

While they were waiting for the report to be
printed, the convention took up the document to
accompany the constitution and with some slight
changes in wording approved it. The draft of
this is in the handwriting of Gouverneur Morris
and presumably was composed by him. It took
the form of a letter to congress, and in general
terms stated the problem before the convention
and why it had been necessary to develop "a different organization" of government. The difficulties encountered were hinted at, and "thus the
Constitution, which we now present, is the result
of a spirit of amity and of that mutual deference
and concession which the peculiarity of our political situation rendered indispensable." The
constitution was not perfect but that "it may
promote the lasting welfare of that country so
dear to us all, and secure her freedom and
happiness, is our most ardent wish."

Another point discussed was the overruling of
the president's veto, which a month before had
been changed from a two-thirds to a three-
fourths vote. Williamson, who had suggested the
previous change, now proposed to change back
again, as he was convinced two-thirds was the

better proportion. Sherman, Gerry, Mason, and Pinckney supported him, while Gouverneur Morris, Hamilton, and Madison spoke in opposition. Madison evidently considered the point of some importance, for he explained that three-fourths was agreed to when the president was to be elected by the legislature and for seven years, whereas now he was to be elected by the people and for four years. The two objects of the veto were to defend the executive rights, and "to prevent popular or factious injustice." The experience of the states had demonstrated that their checks were insufficient. On the whole he concluded that the "danger from the weakness of two-thirds" was greater than the "danger from the strength of three-fourths." In spite of his plea, the change back to two-thirds was made by a vote of six states against four, with one state divided. Madison took pains to record that while Maryland voted for two-thirds, McHenry of that state voted against it, and that the vote of Virginia in the negative was determined by Washington, Blair, and himself overruling Mason and Randolph.

Williamson had been a member of the committee on the unfinished parts of the constitution. It is possible that he had failed to get the committee to report certain changes that he wanted and so now appealed to the convention. At any

rate, having succeeded in obtaining a change in
the provisions concerning the veto he now called
attention to the fact of there being no provision
for juries in civil cases. The records of this discussion are meager and would not be worthy of
notice, had not the point called out so much
criticism later. From the few statements made
in convention and the many explanations made
afterwards, there can be little doubt that there
was no objection to juries in civil cases. The
difficulty came in attempting to lay down a general rule. The practice in the different states
varied, and there were some equity and maritime
cases in which juries were not advisable. As a
matter of fact, the convention was in a hurry to
get through. The end was actually in sight, and
the members did not see how there could be any
danger if the matter were left for congress to
attend to. Accordingly nothing was done.

Even Mason consented to the matter being
passed over, especially if some "general principles" were laid down. Doubtless with his
beloved Virginia bill of rights in mind, he now
expressed the wish that the constitution might be
prefaced with a similar declaration and he claimed
that it would only take a few hours to prepare it.
Gerry promptly moved for a committee to prepare a bill of rights. Sherman is the only one
recorded as speaking against it, and he merely

said that he thought it unnecessary, as the state bills of rights were sufficient and they would not be repealed by the constitution. The convention voted unanimously against the proposal.

Mason then asked to have the prohibition of export taxes reconsidered and when this was granted, he moved that the restriction should not prevent a state from laying duties on exports for the sole purpose of meeting the expenses of inspection, packing, and storing. There was a little discussion of this point, but there seemed to be no serious objection to it provided the power was sufficiently safeguarded. This was accomplished by rendering all such regulations subject to the revision and control of congress. The proviso was then adopted by a large majority.

On Thursday morning, September 13, the printed copies of the report of the committee of style and revision were ready, but before they could be taken up, Mason "after descanting on the extravagance of our manners, the excessive consumption of foreign superfluities, and the necessity of restricting it, as well with œconomical as republican views, . . . moved that a Committee be appointed to report articles of Association for encouraging by the advice the influence and the example of the members of the Convention, œconomy frugality and american manufactures." Doctor Johnson courteously

seconded the motion, and with what was evidently
some impatience the convention agreed to it and
appointed a committee of five, but no report was
ever presented.

Three days were spent by the convention in
carefully comparing each article and section of
the revised draft of the constitution reported by
the committee of style with the proceedings
referred to the committee. In general, the convention heartily approved of the work that had
been done, although as already stated a few dis-
gruntled members afterwards complained of
sharp practices. Even if there were some slight
basis for such charges, the real ground for com-
plaint lay in the fact that the great majority of
the delegates were in favor of the document as it
stood and were impatient at the few members
who were delaying the completion of the work
with what appeared to most of them as only
trivial matters. One finds this sort of a record,
"a number of members being very impatient
and calling for the question" the motion was
promptly voted down.

On the other hand, it was desired that the final
action of the convention should be unanimous.
Accordingly, many concessions were made to conciliate the opposition provided no important
principles were involved. For example, the ultimate congressional control of the time, place, and

manner of holding the election of senators and representatives was limited by inserting " 'except as to the places of choosing Senators' . . . in order to exempt the seats of Government in the States from the power of Congress." The prohibition of a capitation tax was made to include any "other direct tax." Accounts of public receipts and expenditures were ordered to be published from time to time. Prohibition of state laws impairing the obligation of contracts, formerly asked for unavailingly by Rufus King, had been inserted by the committee of style of which he was a member and was now accepted by the convention without question. The appointment of a treasurer by joint ballot of congress was also struck out as making an unfortunate distinction between that officer and others, although Gorham and King thought that the people were accustomed to having treasurers appointed in that way and that the innovation would "multiply objections to the System."

These and other changes were made to conciliate the opposition in the convention, but with a realization that the objections made there were probably the very ones that would be made when the constitution came before the people. Some changes, however, were refused. Requiring a two-thirds vote for navigation acts before 1808 was defeated by seven states against three. A proposal to allow an additional member in the first congress to North Carolina and a similar increase as a sort of bribe to Rhode Island was voted down. A declaration for freedom of the press was thought to be unnecessary, as the power of congress did not extend to the press. A power to establish a national university free from religious distinctions was considered to be included in the power over the seat of government, it being assumed that that was where it would be located. Franklin wanted a specific power in congress to construct canals. Madison wished this to be a general power "to incorporate," with the direct object of providing for internal improvements. Objection was made that the people in New York and Philadelphia would interpret this to mean an intention of establishing a bank and that in other places they would think it was intended to establish mercantile monopolies. The canals being regarded as a concrete case and of the greatest importance, a question limited to that specific case was taken, and only Pennsylvania, Virginia, and Georgia voted for it. Some slight changes were made in the method of amending the constitution, with an idea of making that process easier, but they have proven to be of no importance, because of the difficulty in overcoming the fundamental requirement of obtaining the ratification of three-fourths of the states. It was also feared that congress might refuse to act and so congress was *required* to call a convention on the application of two-thirds of the states. Some further suggestions were made by Sherman, Gerry, and Brearley regarding amendments which were all voted down. But with the idea of conciliation in mind Gouverneur Morris made a motion which was "dictated by the circulating murmurs of the small States . . . that no State, without its consent shall be deprived of its equal suffrage in the Senate."

The articles of confederation formed an agreement "between the States of New Hampshire, Massachusetts, Rhode Island, . . ." and the rest of the thirteen. At one stage of the development of its report, the committee of detail tried in the preamble "We the People of *and* the States of New Hampshire, Massachusetts, Rhode Island," etc., but later the "and" was dropped out. When the committee of style took up this point they found themselves confronted with a new difficulty. The convention had voted that the new constitution might be ratified by nine states and should go into effect between the states so ratifying, and no human power could name those states in advance. How far this was the controlling factor and what other motives may have been at work, we have no record. The simple fact remains that the committee of style cleverly avoided the difficulty before them by phrasing the preamble:—"We, the People of the United States."

Viewed in this light the preamble loses something of the importance often ascribed to it, and yet the opening words remain among the most significant in the constitution. Such a phrase would have been impossible at the beginning of the convention; it was accepted without question at the end. The convention had come together to revise the articles of confederation; it ended by framing an entirely new instrument, the Constitution of the United States.

It was on Saturday, the 15th of September, that the real work of the convention was brought to a close and in order to finish it up the convention continued in session on that day until six o'clock. At that hour Madison's simple statement is: "On the question to agree to the Constitution, as amended. All the States ay.—The Constitution was then ordered to be engrossed."

Just before the vote was taken to agree to the constitution, Randolph made a last plea for a second convention to act upon amendments that might be suggested by individual state conventions. Unless this were done, he said that he could not sign the constitution then and that he might oppose its adoption later. Mason followed in the same vein, and announced that unless a second convention were agreed to, he would neither sign the constitution then, nor give it his support later in Virginia. Gerry also stated his objections to the constitution, and thought that the best thing that could be done was to call a second convention. But the rest of the delegates did not agree with these three men. In view of the troubles they themselves had had, it seemed doubtful that a second convention, coming together after discordant instructions from their constituents, could agree upon anything at all. Accordingly, Randolph's proposal was rejected unanimously.

On Monday, the 17th, the convention met for the last time. The engrossed constitution was read and in order to disguise the fact that a few of the delegates present were unwilling to sign the document, Gouverneur Morris devised a form that would make the action appear to be unanimous: "Done in Convention, by the unanimous consent of *the States* present the 17th of September . . . In Witness whereof we have hereunto subscribed our names." Thinking that the idea would meet with a better reception if it came from some one else than himself, Morris persuaded Franklin to present the proposed form of approval, which Franklin did in a speech urging harmony and unanimity. Franklin himself was rather proud of this effort, and he made several copies of the speech which he sent to various friends. It was not long before the speech found its way into print, and was very favorably received. Another point of view with regard to it, however, which also throws some light upon the contemporary opinion of Franklin, is represented by the note made by McHenry: "It was plain, insinuating persuasive—and in any event of the system guarded the Doctor's fame."

Just before the question was to be put upon the adoption of the engrossed constitution, Gorham said that if it was not too late he would like to see the ratio of representation in the lower house changed from one for every 40,000 inhabitants to one for every 30,000. He was supported by King and Carroll, but there is no reason for supposing that this suggestion would have met with any different fate now than when previously made in the convention, especially as it was so irregular to bring it up at this stage of the proceedings, unless the motion was "inspired." When Washington arose to put the question he said that although he recognized the impropriety of his speaking from the chair he felt this amendment to be of so much consequence that "he could not forbear expressing his wish that the alteration proposed might take place." Without a single objection being made, the change was then unanimously agreed to. This was another concession made to forestall popular criticism, but it may have originated in a suggestion from Washington and under any circumstances its adoption was a striking testimony to his influence.

The constitution was then signed by all the members present, except Gerry, Mason, and Randolph. "Whilst the last members were signing it Doctor Franklin looking towards the Presidents Chair, at the back of which a rising sun happened to be painted, observed to a few members near him, that Painters had found it difficult to distinguish in their art a rising from a setting sun. I have, said he, often and often in the course of the Session, and the vicissitudes of my hopes and fears as to its issue, looked at that behind the President without being able to tell whether it was rising or setting: But now at length I have the happiness to know that it is a rising and not a setting Sun."

It was agreed that the papers of the convention should be turned over to Washington for safe keeping subject to the order of congress if ever formed under the new constitution. The convention then adjourned *sine die*. According to the local papers, the work was completed about four o'clock on Monday afternoon, and from the diary of Washington we know that the "members adjourned to the City Tavern, dined together and took a cordial leave of each other." The next day's edition of the *Pennsylvania Packet and Daily Advertiser* consisted of nothing but the new constitution printed in large type. In those days of limited journalism, there could be no better indication of contemporary opinion as to the importance of what the federal convention had accomplished.

CHAPTER XIII

THE COMPLETED CONSTITUTION

The convention was over; it had completed its work. In the achievement of its task James Madison had been unquestionably the leading spirit. It might be said that he was the master-builder of the constitution. This is not an over-valuation of his services derived from his own account of the proceedings in convention, for Madison laid no undue emphasis upon the part he himself played; in fact, he understated it. Nor is it intended to belittle the invaluable services of many other delegates. But when one studies the contemporary conditions, and tries to discover how well the men of that time grasped the situation; and when one goes farther and, in the light of our subsequent knowledge, seeks to learn how wise were the remedies they proposed,—Madison stands pre-eminent. He seems to have lacked imagination, but this very lack made his work of peculiar value at the moment. His remedies for the unsatisfactory state of affairs under the con-federation, were not founded on theoretical speculations, they were practical. They were in accord with the historical development of our country and in keeping with the genius of our institutions. The evidence is also strong that Madison not only took an important part in the debates but that he was actually looked up to by both friends and opponents as the leader of those in the convention who were in favor of a strong national government.

In these respects, he was in marked contrast to Alexander Hamilton, who was a stronger man intellectually, and suggested a more logical and consistent plan of government than the one which was followed. But Hamilton was out of touch with the situation. He was aristocratic rather than democratic, and while his ideas may have been excellent, they were too radical for the convention and found but little support. At the same time, being in favor of a strong national government, he tried to aid that movement in every way that he could. But within his delegation he was outvoted by Yates and Lansing, and before the sessions were half over he was deprived of a vote altogether by the withdrawal of his colleagues. Finding himself of little service he went to New York and only returned to Philadelphia once or twice for a few days and to sign the completed document in September.

Second to Madison and almost on a par with him was James Wilson. In some respects he was Madison's intellectual superior, but in the immediate work before them he was not as adaptable and not as practical. Still he was Madison's ablest supporter. He appreciated the importance of laying the foundations of the new government broad and deep, and he believed that this could only be done by basing it upon the people themselves. This was the principal thing for which he contended in the convention, and with a great measure of success. His work on the committee of detail was less conspicuous but was also of the greatest service.

Next to these two men should come Washington. Not that he ever spoke in the convention, beyond the one recorded instance at the close of the sessions. But as previously pointed out, personal influence must have been an important factor in the outcome of the convention's work, and Washington's support or opposition would be of the greatest importance. He voted with the Virginia delegation, his views were known, and it is therefore a matter of no little moment that Washington's support was given to Madison. Madison's ideas were the predominating factor in the framing of the constitution and it seems hardly too much to say that Washington's influence, however it may have been exerted, was important and perhaps decisive in determining the acceptance of those ideas by the convention.

Gouverneur Morris was a conspicuous mem-

ber, brilliant but erratic. While he supported
the efforts for a strong national government, his
support was not always a great help. His best
work in the convention was as the member of the
committee on style and arrangement to whom
was entrusted the final drafting of the constitution. Charles Pinckney also took a conspicuous
part in the convention, but his work is not to be
classed with that of other and larger minds. It
is undoubtedly true that he suggested a great
many things that were embodied in the constitution, but they were minor points and details
rather than large, constructive features.

Other members of the convention who deserve
notice, though hardly to be classed with the
names already mentioned, were Rufus King,
General Charles C. Pinckney, John Rutledge,
Nathaniel Gorham and, in spite of their refusal
to sign the completed constitution, Edmund
Randolph and George Mason. It may seem
surprising that no particular mention is made of
Benjamin Franklin, but it must be remembered
that Franklin was at that time a very old man, so
feeble that Wilson read all of his speeches for
him, and while he was highly respected his opinions do not seem to have carried much weight.
For instance, Madison recorded with regard to
one of Franklin's motions: "It was treated with
great respect, but rather for the author of it, than

from any apparent conviction of its expediency or practicability."

Thus far the men who have been considered were all supporters to a greater or less extent of a strong national government. On the other hand were men such as William Paterson, John Dickinson, Elbridge Gerry, Luther Martin, and the three Connecticut delegates, Oliver Ellsworth, William Samuel Johnson, and Roger Sherman. They were fearful of establishing a too strongly centralized government, and at one time or another were to be found in the opposition to Madison and his supporters. They must none the less be given great credit for the form which the constitution finally assumed. They were not mere obstructionists and, while not constructive to the extent that Madison and Wilson were constructive, it is certain that the constitution would not have assumed so satisfactory a form if it had not been for the part taken by them. Their best service was rendered in restraining the tendency of the majority to overrule the rights of states and individuals in endeavoring to establish a thoroughly strong government.

The document which the convention presented to congress and to the country as the proposed new constitution for the United States was a surprise to everybody. No one could have foreseen the processes by which it had been constructed, and no one could have foretold the compromises by which the differences of opinion had been reconciled, and accordingly no one could have forecast the result. Furthermore, the construction of the document was unusual. Wilson and the committee of detail, and Gouverneur Morris and the committee of style had done their work remarkably well. Out of what was almost a hodge-podge of resolutions they had made a presentable document, but it was not a logical piece of work. No document originating as this had and developed as this had been developed could be logical or even consistent. That is why every attempted analysis of the constitution has been doomed to failure. From the very nature of its construction the constitution defies analysis upon a logical basis.

There would seem to be only one way to explain and only one way to understand the "bundle of compromises" known as the constitution of the United States. John Quincy Adams described it when he said that it "had been extorted from the grinding necessity of a reluctant nation."[1] The constitution was a practical piece of work for very practical purposes. It was designed to meet certain specific needs. It was the result of an attempt to remedy the de-

[1] *Jubilee of the Constitution,* 1839, p. 55.

fects experienced in the government under the articles of confederation.

A statement has been made as to what the delegates to the federal convention probably considered those defects of the confederation to be. We have seen that in the speech with which he opened the main business of the convention, Randolph pointed out the most glaring of these defects, and that he presented the Virginia plan as a basis of procedure in providing a remedy for those defects. We have seen how the Virginia plan developed step by step into the constitution. At every stage, suggestions for further remedies were made from one or another delegate, until every defect recorded as known to the members of the convention had been under consideration.

In the completed constitution: the president had been given the power of veto instead of establishing a council of revision; the federal courts instead of congress were to be relied upon to check improper state legislation; and no specific powers had been vested in congress to establish a national bank, to make internal improvements, or to legislate upon the subject of education. With these few exceptions, every known defect of the confederation had been provided for.

On the other hand, there is practically nothing in the constitution that did not arise out of the correction of these specific defects of the confederation. The completed constitution necessarily included many details that would not be mentioned in any enumeration of defects. Compromises had been necessary at every point, and those compromises in some cases produced unforeseen results. With those two qualifications, it would seem to be a safe statement that the only new element in the constitution, that is, the only thing not originating in the correction of the defects noted, was the provision regarding impeachment. This was such a natural result when a powerful executive had been established, that it is hardly worthy of record. It was as inevitable as it was to place limitations upon the extensive powers of congress in order to prevent abuse. When once prescribed for the president, it was but a step to include the "Vice President and all civil Officers."

It has long been recognized that the framers of the constitution were indebted to the constitutions of the individual states for many of the specific provisions in the federal instrument. But this becomes more significant in the light of the present study. However much the members of the federal convention may have prepared themselves by reading and study, and however learnedly they might discourse upon governments, ancient and modern, when it came to concrete action they relied almost entirely upon what they themselves had seen and done. They were dependent upon their experience under the state constitutions and the articles of confederation. John Dickinson expressed this very succinctly in the course of the debates, when he said: "Experience must be our only guide. Reason may mislead us." In fact, making allowance for the compromises and remembering that the state constitutions were only a further development of colonial governments, it is possible to say that every provision of the federal constitution can be accounted for in American experience between 1776 and 1787.

The lack of power to establish a national bank was one of the weaknesses charged against the government of the confederation. It was not specifically provided for in the new constitution, because its importance had not yet been realized. Hamilton's genius, within a year or two, was able to wrest its concession from a reluctant congress, but it required the disastrous financial situation in the War of 1812 to awaken the nation to the necessity of some such institution. In the same way, it was the unexampled spread of population beyond the Alleghanies, and the consequent necessity of better means of transportation, that brought the opposition to acquiesce in national support of internal improvements, which Washington had advocated long before the federal convention met. Gouverneur Morris claimed to have foreseen the acquisition of Louisiana and Canada and to have embodied in the constitution a guarded phrase which would permit of their retention as "provinces, and allow them no voice in our councils." He claimed that "had it been more pointedly expressed, a strong opposition would have been made." Whether or not the people of the United States in 1803 would have accepted Morris' point of view and granted the power he had advocated in 1787, the incident shows the subterfuges to which a far-sighted member of the federal convention resorted in order to provide for possible contingencies beyond the ken of his fellow delegates.

If, then, the federal constitution was nothing but the application of experience to remedy a series of definite defects in the government under the articles of confederation, it must needs be that in the short space of time the confederation had existed experience could not have covered the whole range of governmental activities. Reference is not made here to contingencies impossible to foresee, such as the introduction of steam and electricity, but there were matters that it would seem inexplicable not to have provided for in an instrument of government, if the attempt had been made to frame a logical and comprehensive constitution.

The embargo of 1807 and the protective tariff of 1816 afford illustrations of matters outside the experience of the confederation and not having been expressly provided for in the new instrument raised many doubts as to their constitutionality. The great issue of states rights came forward most dramatically in the concrete cases of nullification and secession. It would have been inexpedient to have forced this issue in 1787, when the fate of any sort of a central government was doubtful. But these subjects were probably not even seriously considered at that time; there certainly is no record of their being mentioned in the convention. Yet it is inconceivable that if Madison, or Wilson, or Hamilton had been permitted to frame a logical or consistent instrument of government, a constitution would have resulted which would not have covered such contingencies. It would seem, then, that the omissions in the constitution furnish a striking proof of its immediately practical character.

Robert Morris took no active part in the proceedings of the convention, but having followed everything that was done with the keenest interest, he wrote to a friend: "This paper has been the subject of infinite investigation, disputation, and declamation. While some have boasted it as a work from Heaven, others have given it a less righteous origin. I have many reasons to believe that it is the work of plain, honest men, and such, I think, it will appear."

It was this compelling feature, its simplicity, its practical character, that was responsible for the final adoption of the constitution when it was laid before the people of the various states. Here was a document which every one could understand. There were differences of opinion, of course, for such differences are inevitable in human nature, and convictions were as strong then as they are now. "In Halifax, Virginia, it is reported that a preacher on a Sunday morning had pronounced from the desk a fervent prayer for the adoption of the federal constitution; but he had no sooner ended his prayer than a clever layman ascended the pulpit, invited the people to join a second time in the supplication, and put forth an animated petition that the new scheme be rejected." Moreover, there is no doubt that the same class of men who may be regarded as responsible for the calling of the federal convention are also to be credited with getting the new constitution adopted. But public opinion, at least so far as it was represented in the state conventions, was divided, and some had to be won over. The substance of the argument which prevailed was: Reform is necessary; the new constitution proposes remedies with which all are familiar; and if the government does not work well, provision is made for changes at any time and to any extent.

Once adopted, the constitution succeeded beyond the hopes of its most ardent advocates. This of course was attributed to virtues inherent in the instrument itself. Respect and admiration developed and quickly grew into what has been well termed "the worship of the constitution." It was this attitude that for so long obscured the insight into the real character of the document. And yet, soon after the federal convention was over, Madison himself had stated in the *Federalist:* "The truth is, that the great principles of the Constitution proposed by the convention may be considered less as absolutely new, than as the expansion of principles which are found in the Articles of Confederation. . . . If the new Constitution be examined with accuracy and candor, it will be found that the change which it proposes consists much less in the addition of *New Powers* to the *Union,* than in the invigoration of its *Original Powers.*"

The articles of confederation had failed; the constitution succeeded. The former worked through the medium of the state governments; the latter by virtue of the power of taxation and of control over commerce, dealt directly with the people. But changes of that sort might have been engrafted upon the old confederation, without so essentially altering its character. Something more was necessary, and something more had been achieved.

A fundamental objection to the old confederation was the inability of congress to enforce its decrees. To remedy this had been one of the chief concerns of the federal convention. The most obvious provision was the power granted to congress "to provide for calling forth the Militia to execute the Laws of the Union." But the most significant provision was the clause originating with Luther Martin and modified by the committee of style to read, "This Constitution . . . shall be the supreme Law of the Land." Not a treaty, nor an agreement between sovereign states, but a law. It was a law enacted by the highest of all law-making bodies, the people; and in its enforcement the government was backed by all the armed power of the nation; but the significance is that it was a law, and as such was enforceable in the courts.

Still this was not enough. Over one hundred years before, in the preface to the *Frame of Government of Pensilvania,* William Penn had quaintly said: "Governments, like clocks, go from the motion men give them; and as governments are made and moved by men, so by them they are ruined too. Wherefore governments rather depend upon men than men upon governments." However radical the differences between the federal constitution and the articles of confederation, however sweeping the provisions of the later document and however carefully they might be worded, the most potent factor in rendering the new instrument of government effective was the changed attitude of the American people. When the federal convention had been called, trade was already improving though it was almost unnoticed. By the time the constitution was adopted and put into operation, the improved conditions were plainly felt. And so it came about that in place of opposition or distrust, commercial confidence caused welcome and support to be extended to the new government.

Neither a work of divine origin, nor "the greatest work that was ever struck off at a given time by the brain and purpose of man," but a practical, workable document is this constitution of the United States. Planned to meet certain immediate needs and modified to suit the exigencies of the situation, it was floated on a wave of commercial prosperity, and it has been adapted by an ingenious political people to meet the changing requirements of a century and a quarter.

APPENDIX

I

THE ARTICLES OF CONFEDERATION[1]

To ALL TO WHOM these Presents shall come, we the undersigned Delegates of the States affixed to our Names send greeting. Whereas the Delegates of the United States of America in Congress assembled did on the fifteenth day of November in the Year of Our Lord One thousand seven Hundred and Seventy seven, and in the second Year of the Independence of America agree to certain articles of Confederation and perpetual Union between the States of Newhamp-shire, Massachusetts-bay, Rhodeisland and Providence Plantations, Connecticut, New York, New Jersey, Penn-sylvania, Delaware, Maryland, Virginia, North-Carolina, South-Carolina, and Georgia in the Words follow-ing, viz. "ARTICLES OF CONFEDERATION and perpetual Union between the States of Newhampshire, Massa-chusetts-bay, Rhodeisland and Providence Plantations, Connecticut, New-York, New-Jersey, Pennsylvania, Delaware, Maryland, Virginia, North-Carolina, South-Carolina and Georgia.

[1] Text taken from *American History Leaflets*, No. 20, and stated to have been copied directly from the original manuscripts.

THE FRAMING OF THE CONSTITUTION

ARTICLE I. THE Stile of this confederacy shall be "THE UNITED STATES OF AMERICA."

ARTICLE II. EACH state retains its sovereignty, freedom and independence, and every Power, Jurisdiction and right, which is not by this confederation expressly delegated to the United States, in Congress assembled.

ARTICLE III. THE said states hereby severally enter into a firm league of friendship with each other, for their common defence, the security of their Liberties, and their mutual and general welfare, binding themselves to assist each other, against all force offered to, or attacks made upon them, or any of them, on account of religion, sovereignty, trade, or any other pretence whatever.

ARTICLE IV. THE better to secure and perpetuate mutual friendship and intercourse among the people of the different states in this union, the free inhabitants of each of these states, paupers, vagabonds, and fugitives from Justice excepted, shall be entitled to all privileges and immunities of free citizens in the several states; and the people of each state shall have free ingress and regress to and from any other state, and shall enjoy therein all the privileges of trade and commerce, subject to the same duties, impositions and restrictions as the inhabitants thereof respectively, provided that such restriction shall not extend so far as to prevent the removal of property imported into any state, to any other state of which the Owner is an inhabitant; provided also that no imposition, duties or restriction shall be laid by any state, on the property of the united states, or either of them.

APPENDIX

IF any Person be guilty of, or charged with treason, felony, or other high misdemeanor in any state, shall flee from Justice, and be found in any of the united states, he shall upon demand of the Governor or executive power, of the state from which he fled, be delivered up and removed to the state having jurisdiction of his offence.

FULL faith and credit shall be given in each of these states to the records, acts and judicial proceedings of the courts and magistrates of every other state.

ARTICLE V. FOR the more convenient management of the general interest of the united states, delegates shall be annually appointed in such manner as the legislature of each state shall direct, to meet in Congress on the first Monday in November, in every year, with a power reserved to each state, to recal its delegates, or any of them, at any time within the year, and to send others in their stead, for the remainder of the Year.

No state shall be represented in Congress by less than two, nor by more than seven Members; and no person shall be capable of being a delegate for more than three years in any term of six years; nor shall any person, being a delegate, be capable of holding any office under the united states, for which he, or another for his benefit receives any salary, fees or emolument of any kind.

EACH state shall maintain its own delegates in a meeting of the states, and while they act as members of the committee of the states.

IN determining questions in the united states, in Congress assembled, each state shall have one vote.

FREEDOM of speech and debate in congress shall not

be impeached or questioned in any Court, or place out of Congress, and the members of Congress shall be protected in their persons from arrests and imprisonments, during the time of their going to and from, and attendance on congress, except for treason, felony, or breach of the peace.

ARTICLE VI. No state without the consent of the united states in congress assembled, shall send any embassy to, or receive any embassy from, or enter into any conference, agreement, alliance or treaty with any King prince or state; nor shall any person holding any office of profit or trust under the united states, or any of them, accept of any present, emolument, office or title of any kind whatever from any king, prince or foreign state; nor shall the united states in congress assembled, or any of them, grant any title of nobility.

No two or more states shall enter into any treaty, confederation or alliance whatever between them, without the consent of the united states in congress assembled, specifying accurately the purpose for which the same is to be entered into, and how long it shall continue.

No state shall lay any imposts or duties, which may interfere with any stipulations in treaties, entered into by the united states in congress assembled, with any king, prince or state, in pursuance of any treaties already proposed by congress, to the courts of France and Spain.

No vessels of war shall be kept up in time of peace by any state, except such number only, as shall be deemed necessary by the united states in congress assembled, for the defence of such state, or its trade; nor shall any body of forces be kept up by any state, in time of peace, except such number only, as in the judgment of the united states, in congress assembled, shall be deemed requisite to garrison the forts necessary for the defence of such state; but every state shall always keep up a well regulated and disciplined militia, sufficiently armed and accoutred, and shall provide and constantly have ready for use, in public stores, a due number of field pieces and tents, and a proper quantity of arms, ammunition and camp equipage.

No state shall engage in any war without the consent of the united states in congress assembled, unless such state be actually invaded by enemies, or shall have received certain advice of a resolution being formed by some nation of Indians to invade such state, and the danger is so imminent as not to admit of a delay, till the united states in congress assembled can be consulted: nor shall any state grant commissions to any ships or vessels of war, nor letters of marque or reprisal, except it be after a declaration of war by the united states in congress assembled, and then only against the kingdom or state and the subjects thereof, against which war has been so declared, and under such regulations as shall be established by the united states in congress assembled, unless such state be infested by pirates, in which case vessels of war may be fitted out for that occasion, and kept so long as the danger shall continue, or until the united states in congress assembled shall determine otherwise.

ARTICLE VII. WHEN land-forces are raised by any state for the common defence, all officers of or under the rank of colonel, shall be appointed by the legislature of each state respectively by whom such forces shall be raised, or in such manner as such state shall direct, and all vacancies shall be filled up by the state which first made the appointment.

ARTICLE VIII. ALL charges of war, and all other expenses that shall be incurred for the common defence or general welfare, and allowed by the united states in congress assembled, shall be defrayed out of a common treasury, which shall be supplied by the several states, in proportion to the value of all land within each state, granted to or surveyed for any Person, as such land and the buildings and improvements thereon shall be estimated according to such mode as the united states in congress assembled, shall from time to time, direct and appoint. The taxes for paying that proportion shall be laid and levied by the authority and direction of the legislatures of the several states within the time agreed upon by the united states in congress assembled.

ARTICLE IX. THE united states in congress assembled, shall have the sole and exclusive right and power of determining on peace and war, except in the cases mentioned in the sixth article—of sending and receiving ambassadors—entering into treaties and alliances, provided that no treaty of commerce shall be made whereby the legislative power of the respective states shall be restrained from imposing such imposts and duties on foreigners, as their own people are subjected to, or from prohibiting the exportation or importation of any species of goods or commodities whatsoever—of establishing rules for deciding in all cases, what captures on land or water shall be legal, and in what manner prizes taken by land or naval forces in the service of the united states shall be divided or appropriated—of granting letters of marque and reprisal in times of peace—appointing courts for the trial of piracies and felonies committed on the high seas and establishing courts for receiving and determining finally appeals in all cases of captures, provided that no member of congress shall be appointed a judge of any of the said courts.

THE united states in congress assembled shall also be the last resort on appeal in all disputes and differences now subsisting or that hereafter may arise between two or more states concerning boundary, jurisdiction or any other cause whatever; which authority shall always be exercised in the manner following. WHENEVER the legislative or executive authority or lawful agent of any state in controversy with another shall present a petition to congress, stating the matter in question and praying for a hearing, notice thereof shall be given by order of congress to the legislative or executive authority of the other state in controversy, and a day assigned for the appearance of the parties by their lawful agents, who shall then be directed to appoint by joint consent, commissioners or judges to constitute a court for hearing and determining the matter in question: but if they cannot agree, congress shall name three persons out of each of the united states, and from the list of such persons each party shall alternately strike out one, the petitioners beginning, until the number shall be reduced to thirteen; and from that number not less than seven, nor more than nine names as congress shall direct, shall in the presence of congress be drawn out by lot, and the persons whose names shall be so drawn or any five of them, shall be commissioners or judges, to hear and finally determine the controversy, so always as a major part of the judges who shall hear the cause shall agree in the determination: and if either party shall neglect to attend at the day appointed, without shewing reasons, which congress shall judge sufficient, or being present shall refuse to strike, the congress shall proceed to nominate three persons out of each state, and the secretary of congress shall strike in behalf of such party absent or refusing; and the judgment and sentence of the court to be appointed, in the manner before prescribed, shall be final and conclusive; and if any of the parties shall refuse to submit to the authority of such court, or to appear or defend their claim or cause, the court shall nevertheless proceed to pronounce sentence, or judgment, which shall in like manner be final and decisive, the judgment or sentence and other proceedings being in either case transmitted to congress, and lodged among the acts of congress for the security of the parties concerned: provided that every commissioner, before he sits in judgment, shall take an oath to be administered by one of the judges of the supreme or superior court of the state, where the cause shall be tried, "well and truly to hear and determine the matter in question, according to the best of his judgment, without favour, affection or hope of reward:" provided also that no state shall be deprived of territory for the benefit of the united states.

APPENDIX

ALL controversies concerning the private right of soil claimed under different grants of two or more states, whose jurisdictions as they may respect such lands, and the states which passed such grants are adjusted, the said grants or either of them being at the same time claimed to have originated antecedent to such settlement of jurisdiction, shall on the petition of either party to the congress of the united states, be finally determined as near as may be in the same manner as is before prescribed for deciding disputes respecting territorial jurisdiction between different states.

THE united states in congress assembled shall also have the sole and exclusive right and power of regulating the alloy and value of coin struck by their own authority, or by that of the respective states—fixing the standard of weights and measures throughout the United States—regulating the trade and manageing all affairs with the Indians, not members of any of the states, provided that the legislative right of any state within its own limits be not infringed or violated—establishing and regulating post-offices from one state to another, throughout all the united states, and exacting such postage on the papers passing thro' the same as may be requisite to defray the expences of the said office—appointing all officers of the land forces, in the service of the united states, excepting regimental officers—appointing all the officers of the naval forces, and commissioning all officers whatever in the service of the united states—making rules for the government and regulation of the said land and naval forces, and directing their operations.

THE united states in congress assembled shall have authority to appoint a committee, to sit in the recess of congress, to be denominated "A Committee of the States," and to consist of one delegate from each state; and to appoint such other committees and civil officers as may be necessary for manageing the general affairs of the united states under their direction—to appoint one of their number to preside, provided that no person be allowed to serve in the office of president more than one year in any term of three years; to ascertain the necessary sums of Money to be raised for the service of the united states, and to appropriate and apply the same for defraying the public expences—to borrow money, or emit bills on the credit of the united states, transmitting every half year to the respective states an account of the sums of money so borrowed or emitted,—to build and equip a navy—to agree upon the number of land forces, and to make requisitions from each state for its quota, in proportion to the number of white inhabitants in such state; which requisition shall be binding, and thereupon the legislature of each state shall appoint the regimental officers, raise the men and cloath, arm and equip them in a soldier like manner, at the expence of the united states; and the officers and men so cloathed, armed and equipped shall march to the place appointed, and within the time agreed on by the united states in congress assembled: But if the united states in congress assembled shall, on consideration of circumstances judge proper that any state should not raise men, or should raise a smaller number than its quota, and that any other state should raise a greater

number of men than the quota thereof, such extra
number shall be raised, officered, cloathed, armed and
equipped in the same manner as the quota of such state,
unless the legislature of such state shall judge that such
extra number cannot be safely spared out of the same,
in which case they shall raise officer, cloath, arm and
equip as many of such extra number as they judge can
be safely spared. AND the officers and men so cloathed,
armed and equipped, shall march to the place appointed,
and within the time agreed on by the united states in
congress assembled.

THE united states in congress assembled shall never
engage in a war, nor grant letters of marque and
reprisal in time of peace, nor enter into any treaties or
alliances, nor coin money, nor regulate the value
thereof, nor ascertain the sums and expences necessary
for the defence and welfare of the united states, or any
of them, nor emit bills, nor borrow money on the credit
of the united states, nor appropriate money, nor agree
upon the number of vessels of war, to be built or purchased, or the number of land or sea forces to be raised,
nor appoint a commander in chief of the army or navy,
unless nine states assent to the same: nor shall a question
on any other point, except for adjourning from day to
day be determined, unless by the votes of a majority of
the united states in congress assembled.

THE congress of the united states shall have power to
adjourn to any time within the year, and to any place
within the united states, so that no period of adjournment be for a longer duration than the space of six
months, and shall publish the Journal of their proceed-

ings monthly, except such parts thereof relating to treaties, alliances or military operations, as in their judgment require secrecy; and the yeas and nays of the delegates of each state on any question shall be entered on the Journal, when it is desired by any delegate; and the delegates of a state, or any of them, at his or their request shall be furnished with a transcript of the said Journal, except such parts as are above excepted, to lay before the legislatures of the several states.

ARTICLE X. THE committee of the states, or any nine of them, shall be authorized to execute, in the recess of congress, such of the powers of congress as the united states in congress assembled, by the consent of nine states, shall from time to time think expedient to vest them with; provided that no power be delegated to the said committee, for the exercise of which, by the articles of confederation, the voice of nine states in the congress of the united states assembled is requisite.

ARTICLE XI. CANADA acceding to this confederation, and joining in the measures of the united states, shall be admitted into, and entitled to all the advantages of this union: but no other colony shall be admitted into the same, unless such admission be agreed to by nine states.

ARTICLE XII. ALL bills of credit emitted, monies borrowed and debts contracted by, or under the authority of congress, before the assembling of the united states, in pursuance of the present confederation, shall be deemed and considered as a charge against the united states, for payment and satisfaction whereof the said united states, and the public faith are hereby solemnly pledged.

ARTICLE XIII. EVERY state shall abide by the determinations of the united states in congress assembled, on all questions which by this confederation are submitted to them. AND the Articles of this confederation shall be inviolably observed by every state, and the union shall be perpetual; nor shall any alteration at any time hereafter be made in any of them; unless such alteration be agreed to in a congress of the united states, and be afterwards confirmed by the legislatures of every state.

AND WHEREAS it hath pleased the Great GOVERNOR of the World to incline the hearts of the legislatures we respectively represent in congress, to approve of, and to authorize us to ratify the said articles of confederation and perpetual union. KNOW YE that we the undersigned delegates, by virtue of the power and authority to us given for that purpose, do by these presents, in the name and in behalf of our respective constituents, fully and entirely ratify and confirm each and every of the said articles of confederation and perpetual union, and all and singular the matters and things therein contained: AND we do further solemnly plight and engage the faith of our respective constituents, that they shall abide by the determinations of the united states in congress assembled, on all questions, which by the said confederation are submitted to them. AND that the articles thereof shall be inviolably observed by the states we respectively represent, and that the union shall be perpetual. IN WITNESS whereof we have hereunto set our hands in Congress. DONE at Philadelphia in the state of Pennsylvania the ninth Day of July in the Year of our Lord one Thousand seven Hundred and Seventy eight, and in the third year of the independence of America.

On the part & behalf of the State of Delaware
{ Thos M: Kean Feb 12. 1779
John Dickinson, May 5th 1779
Nicholas VanDyke, }

on the part and behalf of the State of Maryland
{ John Hanson March 1st 1781
Daniel Carroll. do. }

On the Part and Behalf of the State of Virginia
{ Richard Henry Lee
John Bannister
Thomas Adams
Jno Harvie
Francis Lightfoot Lee }

on the part and Behalf of the State of No. Carolina
{ John Penn July 21st 1778
Corns Harnett
Jno. Williams }

On the part and behalf of the State of South-Carolina
{ Henry Laurens.
William Henry Drayton
Jno. Mathews
Richd. Hudson
Thos. Heyward Junr. }

On the part and behalf of the State of Georgia
{ Jno Walton 24th July 1778
Edwd. Telfair.
Edwd. Langworthy. }

Josiah Bartlett,
John Wentworth Junr
august 8th 1778
} on the part & behalf of the State of New Hampshire

John Hancock.
Samuel Adams
Elbridge Gerry.
Frances Dana
James Lovell
Samuel Holten.
} on the part and behalf of the State of Massachusetts Bay

William Ellery
Henry Marchant
John Collins
} On the part and behalf of the State of Rhode-Island and Providence Plantations

Roger Sherman
Samuel Huntington
Oliver Wolcott
Titus Hosmer
Andrew Adams
} on the Part and behalf of the State of Connecticut

Jas. Duane.
Fras. Lewis
Wm Duer
Gouv. Morris,
} On the Part and Behalf of the State of New York

Jno Witherspoon
Nath. Scudder
} On the Part and in Behalf of the State of New Jersey. Novr. 26. 1778

Robt Morris.
Daniel Roberdeau
Jon. Bayard Smith
William Clingan
Joseph Reed. 22d July 1778
} On the part and behalf of the State of Pennsylvania

APPENDIX

II

THE VIRGINIA PLAN

1. Resolved that the articles of Confederation ought to be so corrected and enlarged as to accomplish the objects proposed by their institution; namely, "common defence, security of liberty and general welfare."

2. Resolved therefore that the rights of suffrage in the National Legislature ought to be proportioned to the Quotas of contribution, or to the number of free inhabitants, as the one or the other rule may seem best in different cases.

3. Resolved that the National Legislature ought to consist of two branches.

4. Resolved that the members of the first branch of the National Legislature ought to be elected by the people of the several States every   for the term of   : to be of the age of   years at least, to receive liberal stipends by which they may be compensated for the devotion of their time to public service; to be incligible to any office established by a particular State, or under the authority of the United States, except those peculiarly belonging to the functions of the first branch, during the term of service, and for the space of   after its expiration; to be incapable of re-election for the space of   after the expiration of their term of service, and to be subject to recall.

5. Resolved that the members of the second branch

of the National Legislature ought to be elected by those of the first, out of a proper number of persons nominated by the individual Legislatures, to be of the age of   years at least; to hold their offices for a term sufficient to ensure their independency, to receive liberal stipends, by which they may be compensated for the devotion of their time to public service; and to be ineligible to any office established by a particular State, or under the authority of the United States, except those peculiarly belonging to the functions of the second branch, during the term of service, and for the space of   after the expiration thereof.

6.   Resolved that each branch ought to possess the right of originating Acts; that the National Legislature ought to be impowered to enjoy the Legislative Rights vested in Congress by the Confederation and moreover to legislate in all cases to which the separate States are incompetent, or in which the harmony of the United States may be interrupted by the exercise of individual Legislation; to negative all laws passed by the several States, contravening in the opinion of the National Legislature the articles of Union; and to call forth the force of the Union against any member of the Union failing to fulfill its duty under the articles thereof.

7.   Resolved that a National Executive be instituted; to be chosen by the National Legislature for the term of   years, to receive punctually at stated times a fixed compensation for the services rendered, in which no increase or diminution shall be made so as to affect the Magistracy, existing at the time of increase

or diminution, and to be incligible a second time; and that besides a general authority to execute the National Laws, it ought to enjoy the Executive rights vested in Congress by the Confederation.

8. Resolved that the Executive and a convenient number of the National Judiciary, ought to compose a council of revision with authority to examine every act of the National Legislature before it shall operate, and every act of a particular Legislature before a Negative thereon shall be final; and that the dissent of the said Council shall amount to a rejection, unless the Act of the National Legislature be again passed, or that of a particular Legislature be again negatived by of the members of each branch.

9. Resolved that a National Judiciary be established to consist of one or more supreme tribunals, and of inferior tribunals to be chosen by the National Legislature, to hold their offices during good behaviour; and to receive punctually at stated times fixed compensation for their services, in which no increase or diminution shall be made so as to affect the persons actually in office at the time of such increase or diminution, that the jurisdiction of the inferior tribunals shall be to hear and determine in the first instance, and of the supreme tribunal to hear and determine in the dernier resort, all piracies and felonies on the high seas, captures from an enemy; cases in which foreigners or citizens of other States applying to such jurisdictions may be interested, or which respect the collection of the National revenue; impeachments of any National

officers, and questions which may involve the national peace and harmony.

10. Resolved that provision ought to be made for the admission of States lawfully arising within the limits of the United States, whether from a voluntary junction of Government and Territory or otherwise, with the consent of a number of voices in the National legislature less than the whole.

11. Resolved that a Republican Government and the territory of each State, except in the instance of a voluntary junction of Government and territory, ought to be guaranteed by the United States to each State

12. Resolved that provision ought to be made for the continuance of Congress and their authorities and privileges, until a given day after the reform of the articles of Union shall be adopted, and for the completion of all their engagements.

13. Resolved that provision ought to be made for the amendment of the Articles of Union whensoever it shall seem necessary, and that the assent of the National Legislature ought not to be required thereto.

14. Resolved that the Legislative Executive and Judiciary powers within the several States ought to be bound by oath to support the articles of Union

15. Resolved that the amendments which shall be offered to the Confederation, by the Convention ought at a proper time, or times, after the approbation of Congress to be submitted to an assembly or assemblies of Representatives, recommended by the several Legislatures to be expressly chosen by the people, to consider and decide thereon.

APPENDIX

III

THE NEW JERSEY PLAN

1. Resolved that the articles of Confederation ought to be so revised, corrected and enlarged, as to render the federal Constitution adequate to the exigencies of Government, and the preservation of the Union.

2. Resolved that in addition to the powers vested in the United States in Congress, by the present existing articles of Confederation, they be authorized to pass acts for raising a revenue, by levying a duty or duties on all goods or merchandizes of foreign growth or manufacture, imported into any part of the United States, by Stamps on paper, vellum or parchment, and by a postage on all letters or packages passing through the general post-Office, to be applied to such federal purposes as they shall deem proper and expedient; to make rules and regulations for the collection thereof; and the same from time to time, to alter and amend in such manner as they shall think proper: to pass Acts for the regulation of trade and commerce as well with foreign nations as with each other: provided that all punishments, fines, forfeitures and penalties to be incurred for contravening such acts rules and regulations shall be adjudged by the Common law Judiciarys of the State in which any offence contrary to the true intent and meaning of such Acts rules and regulations shall have been committed or perpetrated, with liberty of commencing in the first instance all suits and prose-

cutions for that purpose in the superior Common law Judiciary in such State, subject nevertheless, for the correction of all errors, both in law and fact in rendering judgment, to an appeal to the Judiciary of the United States.

3. Resolved that whenever requisitions shall be necessary, instead of the rule for making requisitions mentioned in the articles of Confederation, the United States in Congress be authorized to make such requisitions in proportion to the whole number of white and other free citizens and inhabitants of every age sex and and condition including those bound to servitude for a term of years and three fifths of all other persons not comprehended in the foregoing description, except Indians not paying taxes; that if such requisitions be not complied with, in the time specified therein, to direct the collection thereof in the non complying States and for that purpose to devise and pass acts directing and authorizing the same; provided that none of the powers hereby vested in the United States in Congress shall be exercised without the consent of at least   States, and in that proportion if the number of Confederated States should hereafter be increased or diminished.

4. Resolved that the United States in Congress be authorized to elect a federal Executive to consist of   persons, to continue in office for the term of   years, to receive punctually at stated times a fixed compensation for their services, in which no increase or diminution shall be made so as to affect the persons composing the Executive at the time of such increase or diminution, to be paid out of the federal

treasury; to be incapable of holding any other office or appointment during their time of service and for years thereafter; to be ineligible a second time, and removeable by Congress on application by a majority of the Executives of the several States; that the Executives besides their general authority to execute the federal acts ought to appoint all federal officers not otherwise provided for, and to direct all military operations; provided that none of the persons composing the federal Executive shall on any occasion take command of any troops, so as personally to conduct any enterprise as General, or in other capacity.

5. Resolved that a federal Judiciary be established to consist of a supreme Tribunal the Judges of which to be appointed by the Executive, and to hold their offices during good behaviour, to receive punctually at stated times a fixed compensation for their services in which no increase or diminution shall be made, so as to affect the persons actually in office at the time of such increase or diminution; that the Judiciary so established shall have authority to hear and determine in the first instance on all impeachments of federal officers, and by way of appeal in the dernier resort in all cases touching the rights of Ambassadors, in all cases of captures from an enemy, in all cases of piracies and felonies on the high seas, in all cases in which foreigners may be interested, in the construction of any treaty or treaties, or which may arise on any of the Acts for regulation of trade, or the collection of the federal Revenue: that none of the Judiciary shall during the time they remain in Office be capable of receiving or holding any other

office or appointment during their time of service, or for thereafter.

6. Resolved that all Acts of the United States in Congress made by virtue and in pursuance of the powers hereby and by the articles of confederation vested in them, and all Treaties made and ratified under the authority of the United States shall be the supreme law of the respective States so far forth as those Acts or Treaties shall relate to the said States or their Citizens, and that the Judiciary of the several States shall be bound thereby in their decisions, any thing in the respective laws of the Individual States to the contrary notwithstanding; and that if any State, or any body of men in any State shall oppose or prevent the carrying into execution such acts or treaties, the federal Executive shall be authorized to call forth the power of the Confederated States, or so much thereof as may be necessary to enforce and compel an obedience to such Acts, or an Observance of such Treaties.

7. Resolved that provision be made for the admission of new States into the Union.

8. Resolved the rule for naturalization ought to be the same in every State

9. Resolved that a Citizen of one State committing an offence in another State of the Union, shall be deemed guilty of the same offence as if it had been committed by a Citizen of the State in which the Offence was committed.

APPENDIX

IV

THE CONSTITUTION OF THE UNITED STATES

WE THE PEOPLE of the United States, in Order to form a more perfect Union, establish Justice, insure domestic Tranquility, provide for the common defence, promote the general Welfare, and secure the Blessings of Liberty to ourselves and our Posterity, do ordain and establish this Constitution for the United States of America.

ARTICLE. I.

Section. 1. All legislative Powers herein granted shall be vested in a Congress of the United States, which shall consist of a Senate and House of Representatives.

Section. 2. The House of Representatives shall be composed of Members chosen every second Year by the People of the several States, and the Electors in each State shall have (the) Qualifications requisite for Electors of the most numerous Branch of the State Legislature.

No Person shall be a Representative who shall not have attained to the Age of twenty five Years, and been seven Years a Citizen of the United States, and who shall not, when elected, be an Inhabitant of that State in which he shall be chosen.

Representatives and direct Taxes shall be apportioned among the several States which may be included within this Union, according to their respective Numbers, which shall be determined by adding to the whole Number of free Persons, including those bound to Service for a Term of Years, and excluding Indians not taxed, three fifths of all other Persons. The actual Enumeration shall be made within three Years after the first Meeting of the Congress of the United States, and within every subsequent Term of ten Years, in such Manner as they shall by Law direct. The Number of Representatives shall not exceed one for every (thirty) Thousand, but each State shall have at Least one Representative; and until such enumeration shall be made, the State of New Hampshire shall be entitled to chuse three, Massachusetts eight, Rhode-Island and Providence Plantations one, Connecticut five, New-York six, New Jersey four, Pennsylvania eight, Delaware one, Maryland six, Virginia ten, North Carolina five, South Carolina five, and Georgia three.

When vacancies happen in the Representation from any State, the Executive Authority thereof shall issue Writs of Election to fill such Vacancies.

The House of Representatives shall chuse their Speaker and other Officers; and shall have the sole Power of Impeachment.

Section. 3. The Senate of the United States shall be composed of two Senators from each State, chosen by the Legislature thereof, for six Years; and each Senator shall have one Vote.

Immediately after they shall be assembled in Consequence of the first Election, they shall be divided as equally as may be into three Classes. The Seats of the

Senators of the first Class shall be vacated at the Expiration of the second Year, of the second Class at the Expiration of the fourth Year, and of the third Class at the Expiration of the sixth Year, so that one third may be chosen every second Year; and if Vacancies happen by Resignation, or otherwise, during the Recess of the Legislature of any State, the Executive thereof may make temporary Appointments until the next Meeting of the Legislature, which shall then fill such Vacancies.

No Person shall be a Senator who shall not have attained to the Age of thirty Years, and been nine Years a Citizen of the United States, and who shall not, when elected, be an inhabitant of that State for which he shall be chosen.

The Vice President of the United States shall be President of the Senate, but shall have no Vote, unless they be equally divided.

The Senate shall chuse their other Officers, and also a President pro tempore, in the Absence of the Vice President, or when he shall exercise the Office of President of the United States.

The Senate shall have the sole Power to try all Impeachments. When sitting for that Purpose, they shall be on Oath or Affirmation. When the President of the United States (is tried,) the Chief Justice shall preside: And no Person shall be convicted without the Concurrence of two thirds of the Members present.

Judgment in Cases of Impeachment shall not extend further than to removal from Office, and disqualification to hold and enjoy any Office of honor, Trust or Profit under the United States: but the Party convicted shall nevertheless be liable and subject to Indictment, Trial, Judgment and Punishment, according to Law.

Section. 4. The Times, Places and Manner of holding Elections for Senators and Representatives, shall be prescribed in each State by the Legislature thereof; but the Congress may at any time by Law make or alter such Regulations, except as to the Places of chusing Senators.

The Congress shall assemble at least once in every Year, and such Meeting shall be on the first Monday in December, unless they shall by Law appoint a different Day.

Section. 5. Each House shall be the Judge of the Elections, Returns and Qualifications of its own Members, and a Majority of each shall constitute a Quorum to do Business; but a smaller Number may adjourn from day to day, and may be authorized to compel the Attendance of absent Members, in such Manner, and under such Penalties as each House may provide.

Each House may determine the Rules of its Proceedings, punish its Members for disorderly Behaviour, and, with the Concurrence of two thirds, expel a Member.

Each House shall keep a Journal of its Proceedings, and from time to time publish the same, excepting such Parts as may in their Judgment require Secrecy; and the Yeas and Nays of the Members of either House on any question shall, at the Desire of one fifth of those Present, be entered on the Journal.

Neither House, during the Session of Congress, shall, without the Consent of the other, adjourn for more than three days, nor to any other Place than that in which the two Houses shall be sitting.

Section. 6. The Senators and Representatives shall receive a Compensation for their Services, to be ascertained by Law, and paid out of the Treasury of the United States. They shall in all Cases, except Treason, Felony and Breach of the Peace, be privileged from Arrest during their Attendance at the Session of their respective Houses, and in going to and returning from the same; and for any Speech or Debate in either House, they shall not be questioned in any other Place.

No Senator or Representative shall, during the Time for which he was elected, be appointed to any civil Office under the Authority of the United States, which shall have been created, or the Emoluments whereof shall have been encreased during such time; and no Person holding any Office under the United States, shall be a Member of either House during his Continuance in Office.

Section. 7. All Bills for raising Revenue shall originate in the House of Representatives; but the Senate may propose or concur with Amendments as on other Bills.

Every Bill which shall have passed the House of Representatives and the Senate, shall, before it become a Law, be presented to the President of the United States; If he approve he shall sign it, but if not he shall return it, with his Objections to that House in which it shall have originated, who shall enter the Objections at large on their Journal, and proceed to reconsider it. If after such Reconsideration two thirds of that House shall agree to pass the Bill, it shall be sent, together with the Objections, to the other House, by which it shall likewise be reconsidered, and if approved by two thirds of that House, it shall become a Law. But in all such Cases the Votes of both Houses shall be determined by yeas and Nays, and the Names of the Persons voting for and against the Bill shall be entered on the Journal of each House respectively. If any Bill shall not be returned by the President within ten Days (Sundays excepted) after it shall have been presented to him, the Same shall be a Law, in like Manner as if he had signed it, unless the Congress by their Adjournment prevent its Return, in which Case it shall not be a Law.

Every Order, Resolution, or Vote to which the Concurrence of the Senate and House of Representatives may be necessary (except on a question of Adjournment) shall be presented to the President of the United States; and before the Same shall take Effect, shall be approved by him, or being disapproved by him, shall be repassed by two thirds of the Senate and House of Representatives, according to the Rules and Limitations prescribed in the Case of a Bill.

Section. 8. The Congress shall have Power To lay and collect Taxes, Duties, Imposts and Excises, to pay the Debts and Provide for the common Defence and general Welfare of the United States; but all Duties, Imposts and Excises shall be uniform throughout the United States;

APPENDIX

To borrow Money on the credit of the United States;

To regulate Commerce with foreign Nations, and among the several States, and with the Indian Tribes;

To establish an uniform Rule of Naturalization, and uniform Laws on the subject of Bankruptcies throughout the United States;

To coin Money, regulate the Value thereof, and of foreign Coin, and fix the Standard of Weights and Measures;

To provide for the Punishment of counterfeiting the Securities and current Coin of the United States;

To establish Post Offices and post Roads;

To promote the Progress of Science and useful Arts, by securing for limited Time to Authors and Inventors the exclusive Right to their respective Writings and Discoveries;

To constitute Tribunals inferior to the supreme Court;

To define and punish Piracies and Felonies committed on the high Seas, and Offences against the Law of Nations;

To declare War, grant Letters of Marque and Reprisal, and make Rules concerning Captures on Land and Water;

To raise and support Armies, but no Appropriation of Money to that Use shall be for a longer Term than two Years;

To provide and maintain a Navy;

To make Rules for the Government and Regulation of the land and naval Forces;

To provide for calling forth the Militia to execute

the Laws of the Union, suppress Insurrections and repel Invasions;

To provide for organizing, arming, and disciplining, the Militia, and for governing such Part of them as may be employed in the Service of the United States, reserving to the States respectively, the Appointment of the Officers, and the Authority of training the Militia according to the discipline prescribed by Congress;

To exercise exclusive Legislation in all Cases whatsoever, over such District (not exceeding ten Miles square) as may, by Cession of Particular States, and the Acceptance of Congress, become the Seat of the Government of the United States, and to exercise like Authority over all Places purchased by the Consent of the Legislature of the State in which the Same shall be, for the Erection of Forts, Magazines, Arsenals, dock-Yards, and other needful Buildings;—And

To make all Laws which shall be necessary and proper for carrying into Execution the foregoing Powers, and all other Powers vested by this Constitution in the Government of the United States, or in any Department or Officer thereof.

Section. 9. The Migration or Importation of such Persons as any of the States now existing shall think proper to admit, shall not be prohibited by the Congress prior to the Year one thousand eight hundred and eight, but a Tax or duty may be imposed on such Importation, not exceeding ten dollars for each Person.

The Privilege of the Writ of Habeas Corpus shall not be suspended, unless when in Cases of Rebellion or Invasion the public Safety may require it.

No Bill of Attainder or ex post facto Law shall be passed.

No Capitation, or other direct, Tax shall be laid, unless in Proportion to the Census or Enumeration herein before directed to be taken.

No Tax or Duty shall be laid on Articles exported from any State.

No Preference shall be given by any Regulation of Commerce or Revenue to the Ports of one State over those of another: nor shall Vessels bound to, or from, one State, be obliged to enter, clear, or pay Duties in another.

No Money shall be drawn from the Treasury, but in Consequence of Appropriations made by Law; and a regular Statement and Account of the Receipts and Expenditures of all public Money shall be published from time to time.

No Title of Nobility shall be granted by the United States: And no Person holding any Office of Profit or Trust under them, shall, without (the) Consent of the Congress, accept of any present, Emolument, Office, or Title, of any kind whatever, from any King, Prince, or foreign State.

Section. 10.   No State shall enter into any Treaty, Alliance, or Confederation; grant Letters of Marque and Reprisal; coin Money; emit Bills of Credit; make any Thing but gold and silver Coin a Tender in Payment of Debts; pass any Bill of Attainder, ex post facto Law, or Law impairing the Obligation of Contracts, or grant any Title of Nobility.

No State shall, without the Consent of (the) Congress, lay any Imposts or Duties on Imports or Exports, except what may be absolutely necessary for executing it's inspection Laws: and the net Produce of all Duties and Imposts, laid by any State on Imports or Exports, shall be for the Use of the Treasury of the United States; and all such Laws shall be subject to the Revision and Controul of (the) Congress.

No State shall, without the Consent of Congress, lay any Duty of Tonnage, keep Troops, or Ships of War in time of Peace, enter into any Agreement or Compact with another State, or with a foreign Power, or engage in War, unless actually invaded, or in such imminent Danger as will not admit of delay.

Article. II.

Section. 1. The executive Power shall be vested in a President of the United States of America. He shall hold his Office during the Term of four Years, and, together with the Vice President, chosen for the same Term, be elected, as follows

Each State shall appoint, in such Manner as the Legislature thereof may direct, a Number of Electors, equal to the whole Number of Senators and Representatives to which the State may be entitled in the Congress: but no Senator or Representative, or Person holding an Office of Trust or Profit under the United States, shall be appointed an Elector.

The Electors shall meet in their respective States, and vote by Ballot for two Persons, of whom one at least shall not be an Inhabitant of the same State with themselves. And they shall make a List of all the Persons voted for, and of the Number of Votes for each; which List they shall sign and certify, and transmit sealed to the Seat of the Government of the United States, directed to the President of the Senate. The President of the Senate shall, in the Presence of the Senate and House of Representatives, open all the Certificates, and the Votes shall then be counted. The Person having the greatest Number of Votes shall be the President, if such Number be a Majority of the whole Number of Electors appointed; and if there be more than one who have such Majority, and have an equal Number of Votes, then the House of Representatives shall immediately chuse by Ballot one of them for President; and if no Person have a Majority, then from the five highest on the List the said House shall in like Manner chuse the President. But in chusing the President, the Votes shall be taken by States, the Representation from each State having one Vote; A quorum for this Purpose shall consist of a Member or Members from two thirds of the States, and a Majority of all the States shall be necessary to a Choice. In every Case, after the Choice of the President, the Person having the greatest Number of Votes of the Electors shall be the Vice President. But if there should remain two or more who have equal Votes, the Senate shall chuse from them by Ballot the Vice President.

The Congress may determine the Time of chusing the Electors, and the Day on which they shall give their Votes; which Day shall be the same throughout the United States.

No Person except a natural born Citizen, or a Citizen of the United States, at the time of the Adoption of this Constitution, shall be eligible to the Office of President; neither shall any Person be eligible to that Office who shall not have attained to the Age of thirty five Years, and been fourteen Years a Resident within the United States.

In Case of the Removal of the President from Office, or of his Death, Resignation, or Inability to discharge the Powers and Duties of the said Office, the Same shall devolve on the Vice President, and the Congress may by Law provide for the Case of Removal, Death, Resignation or Inability, both of the President and Vice President, declaring what Officer shall then act as President, and such Officer shall act accordingly, until the Disability be removed, or a President shall be elected.

The President shall, at stated Times, receive for his Services, a Compensation, which shall neither be encreased nor diminished during the Period for which he shall have been elected, and he shall not receive within that Period any other Emolument from the United States, or any of them.

Before he enter on the Execution of his Office, he shall take the following Oath of Affirmation:—"I do solemnly swear (or affirm) that I will faithfully execute the Office of President of the United States, and will to the best of my Ability, preserve, protect and defend the Constitution of the United States."

Section 2. The President shall be Commander in Chief of the Army and Navy of the United States, and of the Militia of the several States, when called into the actual Service of the United States; he may require the Opinion, in writing, of the principal Officer in each of the executive Departments, upon any Subject relating to the Duties of their respective Offices, and he shall have Power to grant Reprieves and Pardons for Offences against the United States, except in Cases of Impeachment.

He shall have Power, by and with the Advice and Consent of the Senate, to make Treaties, provided two thirds of the Senators present concur; and he shall nominate, and by and with the Advice and Consent of the Senate, shall appoint Ambassadors, other public Ministers and Consuls, Judges of the supreme Court, and all other Officers of the United States, whose appointments are not herein otherwise provided for, and which shall be established by Law: but the Congress may by Law vest the Appointment of such inferior Officers, as they think proper, in the President alone, in the Courts of Law, or in the Heads of Departments.

The President shall have Power to fill up all Vacancies that may happen during the Recess of the Senate, by granting Commissions which shall expire at the End of their next Session.

Section. 3. He shall from time to time give to the Congress Information of the State of the Union, and recommend to their consideration such Measures as he shall judge necessary and expedient; he may, on extraordinary Occasions, convene both Houses, or either of them, and in Case of Disagreement between them, with Respect to the Time of Adjournment, he may adjourn them to such Time as he shall think proper; he shall receive Ambassadors and other public Ministers; he shall take Care that the Laws be faithfully executed, and shall Commission all the Officers of the United States.

Section. 4. The President, Vice President and all civil Officers of the United States, shall be removed from Office on Impeachment for, and conviction of, Treason, Bribery, or other high Crimes and Misdemeanors.

ARTICLE. III.

Section 1. The judicial Power of the United States, shall be vested in one supreme Court, and in such inferior Courts as the Congress may from time to time ordain and establish. The Judges, both of the supreme and inferior Courts, shall hold their Offices during good Behaviour, and shall, at stated Times, receive for their Services, a Compensation, which shall not be diminished during their Continuance in Office.

Section 2. The judicial Power shall extend to all Cases, in Law and Equity, arising under this Constitution, the Laws of the United States, and Treaties made, or which shall be made, under their Authority;—to all Cases affecting Ambassadors, other public Ministers and Consuls;—to all Cases of admiralty and maritime Jurisdiction;—to Controversies to which the United States shall be a Party;—to Controversies between two or more States;—between a State and Citizens of another State;—between Citizens of different States,— between Citizens of the same State claiming Lands under

Grants of different States, and between a State, or the Citizens thereof, and foreign States, Citizens or Subjects.

In all Cases affecting Ambassadors, other public Ministers and Consuls, and those in which a State shall be Party, the supreme Court shall have original Jurisdiction. In all the other Cases before mentioned, the supreme Court shall have appellate Jurisdiction, both as to Law and Fact, with such Exceptions, and under such Regulations as the Congress shall make.

The Trial of all Crimes, except in Cases of Impeachment, shall be by Jury; and such Trial shall be held in the State where the said Crimes shall have been committed; but when not committed within any State, the Trial shall be at such Place or Places as the Congress may by Law have directed.

Section. 3. Treason against the United States, shall consist only in levying War against them, or in adhering to their Enemies, giving them Aid and Comfort. No Person shall be convicted of Treason unless on the Testimony of two Witnesses to the same overt Act, or on Confession in open Court.

The Congress shall have Power to declare the Punishment of Treason, but no Attainder of Treason shall work Corruption of Blood, or Forfeiture except during the Life of the Person attainted.

ARTICLE. IV.

Section. 1. Full Faith and Credit shall be given in each State to the public Acts, Records, and judicial Proceedings of every other State. And the Congress may by general Laws prescribe the Manner in which such Acts, Records and Proceedings shall be proved, and the Effect thereof.

Section. 2. The Citizens of each State shall be entitled to all Privileges and Immunities of Citizens in the several States.

A Person charged in any State with Treason, Felony, or other Crime, who shall flee from Justice, and be found in another State, shall on Demand of the executive Authority of the State from which he fled, be delivered up, to be removed to the State having Jurisdiction of the Crime.

No Person held to Service or Labour in one State, under the Laws thereof, escaping into another, shall, in Consequence of any Law or Regulation therein, be discharged from such Service or Labour, but shall be delivered up on Claim of the Party to whom such Service or Labour may be due.

Section. 3. New States may be admitted by the Congress into this Union; but no new State shall be formed or erected within the Jurisdiction of any other State; nor any State be formed by the Junction of two or more States, or Parts of States, without the Consent of the Legislatures of the States concerned as well as of the Congress.

The Congress shall have Power to dispose of and make all needful Rules and Regulations respecting the Territory or other Property belonging to the United States; and nothing in this Constitution shall be so construed as to Prejudice any Claims of the United States, or of any particular State.

Section. 4. The United States shall guarantee to every State in this Union a Republican Form of Government, and shall protect each of them against Invasion; and on Application of the Legislature, or of the Executive (when the Legislature cannot be convened) against domestic Violence.

Article. V.

The Congress, whenever two thirds of both Houses shall deem it necessary, shall propose Amendments to this Constitution, or, on the Application of the Legislatures of two thirds of the several States, shall call a Convention for proposing Amendments, which, in either Case, shall be valid to all Intents and Purposes, as Part of this Constitution, when ratified by the Legislatures of three fourths of the several States, or by Conventions in three fourths thereof, as the one or the other Mode of Ratification may be proposed by the Congress; Provided that no Amendment which may be made prior to the Year One thousand eight hundred and eight shall in any Manner affect the first and fourth Clauses in the Ninth Section of the first Article; and that no State, without its Consent, shall be deprived of it's equal Suffrage in the Senate.

Article. VI.

All Debts contracted and Engagements entered into, before the Adoption of this Constitution, shall be as valid against the United States under this Constitution, as under the Confederation.

THE FRAMING OF THE CONSTITUTION

This Constitution, and the Laws of the United States which shall be made in Pursuance thereof; and all Treaties made, or which shall be made, under the Authority of the United States, shall be the supreme Law of the Land; and the Judges in every State shall be bound thereby, any Thing in the Constitution or Laws of any State to the Contrary notwithstanding.

The Senators and Representatives before mentioned, and the Members of the several State Legislatures, and all executive and judicial Officers, both of the United States and of the several States, shall be bound by Oath or Affirmation, to support this Constitution; but no religious Test shall ever be required as a Qualification to any Office or public Trust under the United States.

ARTICLE. VII.

The Ratification of the Conventions of nine States, shall be sufficient for the Establishment of this Constitution between the States so ratifying the Same.

The Word "the," being interlined between the seventh and eighth Lines of the first Page, the word "Thirty" being partly written on an Erasure in the fifteenth Line of the first Page. The words "is tried" being interlined between the thirty-second and thirty-third Lines of the first Page and the Word "the" being interlined between the

DONE in Convention by the Unanimous Consent of the States present the Seventeenth Day of September in the Year of our Lord one thousand seven hundred and Eighty seven and of the Independence of the

APPENDIX

forty-third and forty-fourth Lines of the second Page. ['I'hese corrections are indicated in the text by parentheses.]

United States of America the Twelfth IN WITNESS whereof We have hereunto subscribed our Names,

Go, Washington—Presidt. and deputy from Virginia.

Delaware	Geo: Read Gunning Bedford jun John Dickinson Richard Bassett Jaco · Broom
Maryland	James McHenry Dan of St Thos. Jenifer Danl. Carroll.
Virginia	John Blair — James Madison Jr.
North Carolina	Wm. Blount Richd. Dobbs Spaight. Hu Williamson
South Carolina	J. Rutledge Charles Cotesworth Pinckney Charles Pinckney Pierce Butler.
Georgia	William Few Abr Baldwin

New Hampshire	John Langdon Nicholas Gilman
Massachusetts	Nathaniel Gorham Rufus King
Connecticut	Wm · Saml. Johnson Roger Sherman
New York . . .	Alexander Hamilton
New Jersey	Wil: Livingston David Brearley. Wm. Paterson. Jona: Dayton
Pennsylvania	B Franklin Thomas Mifflin Robt Morris Geo. Clymer Thos. Fitzsimons Jared Ingersoll James Wilson Gouv Morris

V

THE AMENDMENTS TO THE CONSTITUTION[1]

[ARTICLES in addition to and Amendment of the Constitution of the United States of America, proposed by Congress, and ratified by the Legislatures of the several States, pursuant to the fifth Article of the original Constitution.][2]

[ARTICLE I.][3]

Congress shall make no law respecting an establishment of religion, or prohibiting the free exercise thereof; or abridging the freedom of speech, or of the press; or the right of the people peaceably to assemble, and to petition the Government for a redress of grievances.

[ARTICLE II.]

A well regulated Militia, being necessary to the security of a free State, the right of the people to keep and bear Arms, shall not be infringed.

[1] Texts taken from *American History Leaflets,* No. 8, and stated to have been copied directly from the original manuscripts.

[2] This heading appears only in the joint resolution of congress submitting the first ten amendments.

[3] In the original manuscripts the first twelve amendments have no numbers. The first ten amendments appear to have been in force from November 3, 179'

APPENDIX

[ARTICLE III.]

No Soldier shall, in time of peace be quartered in any house, without the consent of the Owner, nor in time of war, but in a manner to be prescribed by law.

[ARTICLE IV.]

The right of the people to be secure in their persons, houses, papers, and effects, against unreasonable searches and seizures, shall not be violated, and no Warrants shall issue, but upon probable cause, supported by Oath or affirmation, and particularly describing the place to be searched, and the persons or things to be seized.

[ARTICLE V.]

No person shall be held to answer for a capital, or otherwise infamous crime, unless on a presentment or indictment of a Grand Jury except in cases arising in the land or naval forces, or in the Militia, when in actual service in time of War or public danger; nor shall any person be subject for the same offence to be twice put in jeopardy of life or limb; nor shall be compelled in any criminal case to be a witness against himself, nor be deprived of life, liberty, or property, without due process of law; nor shall private property be taken for public use, without just compensation.

[ARTICLE VI.]

In all criminal prosecutions the accused shall enjoy the right to a speedy and public trial, by an impartial jury of the State and district wherein the crime shall have been committed, which district shall have been previously ascertained by law, and to be informed of the nature and cause of the accusation; to be confronted with the witnesses against him; to have compulsory process for obtaining witnesses in his favor, and to have the Assistance of Counsel for his defence.

[ARTICLE VII.]

In suits at common law, where the value in controversy shall exceed twenty dollars, the right of trial by jury shall be preserved, and no fact tried by a jury shall be otherwise re-examined in any Court of the United States, than according to the rules of the common law.

[ARTICLE VIII.]

Excessive bail shall not be required, nor excessive fines imposed, nor cruel and unusual punishments inflicted.

[ARTICLE IX.]

The enumeration in the Constitution, of certain rights, shall not be construed to deny or disparage others retained by the people.

[ARTICLE X.]

The powers not delegated to the United States by the Constitution, nor prohibited by it to the States, are reserved to the States respectively or to the people.

APPENDIX

[ARTICLE XI.][4]

The Judicial power of the United States shall not be construed to extend to any suit in law or equity, commenced or prosecuted against one of the United States by Citizens of another State, or by Citizens or Subjects of any Foreign State.

[ARTICLE XII.][5]

The Electors shall meet in their respective states, and vote by ballot for President and Vice-President, one of whom, at least, shall not be an inhabitant of the same state with themselves; they shall name in their ballots the person voted for as President, and in distinct ballots the person voted for as Vice-President, and they shall make distinct lists of all persons voted for as President, and of all persons voted for as Vice-President, and of the number of votes for each, which lists they shall sign and certify, and transmit sealed to the seat of the government of the United States, directed to the President of the Senate;—The President of the Senate shall, in the presence of the Senate and House of Representatives, open all the certificates and the votes shall then be counted;—The person having the greatest number of votes for President, shall be the President, if such number be a majority of the whole number of Electors appointed; and if no person have such majority, then from the persons having the highest numbers not exceeding three on the list of those voted for as President, the House of Representatives shall choose imme-

4 Proclaimed to be in force January 8, 1798.
5 Proclaimed to be in force September 25, 1804.

diately, by ballot, the President. But in choosing the President, the votes shall be taken by states, the representation from each state having one vote; a quorum for this purpose shall consist of a member or members from two-thirds of the states, and a majority of all the states shall be necessary to a choice. And if the House of Representatives shall not choose a President whenever the right of choice shall devolve upon them, before the fourth day of March next following, then the Vice-President shall act as President, as in the case of the death or other constitutional disability of the President. —The person having the greatest number of votes as Vice-President, shall be the Vice-President, if such number be a majority of the whole number of Electors appointed, and if no person have a majority, then from the two highest numbers on the list, the Senate shall choose the Vice-President; a quorum for the purpose shall consist of two-thirds of the whole number of Senators, and a majority of the whole number shall be necessary to a choice. But no person constitutionally ineligible to the office of President shall be eligible to that of Vice-President of the United States.

ARTICLE XIII.[6]

SECTION 1. Neither slavery nor involuntary servitude, except as a punishment for crime whereof the party shall have been duly convicted, shall exist within the United States, or any place subject to their jurisdiction. SECTION 2. Congress shall have power to enforce this article by appropriate legislation.

6 Proclaimed to be in force December 18, 1865.

APPENDIX

ARTICLE XIV.[7]

SECTION 1.   All persons born or naturalized in the United States, and subject to the jurisdiction thereof, are citizens of the United States and of the State wherein they reside.   No State shall make or enforce any law which shall abridge the privileges or immunities of citizens of the United States; nor shall any State deprive any person of life, liberty, or property, without due process of law; nor deny to any person within its jurisdiction the equal protection of the laws.

SECTION 2.   Representatives shall be apportioned among the several States according to their respective numbers, counting the whole number of persons in each State, excluding Indians not taxed.   But when the right to vote at any election for the choice of electors for President and Vice-President of the United States, Representatives in Congress, the Executive and Judicial officers of a State, or the members of the Legislature thereof, is denied to any of the male inhabitants of such State, being twenty-one years of age, and citizens of the United States, or in any way abridged, except for participation in rebellion, or other crime, the basis of representation therein shall be reduced in the proportion which the number of such male citizens shall bear to the whole number of male citizens twenty-one years of age in such State.

SECTION 3.   No person shall be a Senator or Representative in Congress, or elector of President and Vice President, or hold any office, civil or military, under the United States, or under any State, who, having pre-

[7] Proclaimed to be in force July 28, 1868.

viously taken an oath, as a member of Congress, or as an officer of the United States, or as a member of any State legislature, or as an executive or judicial officer of any State, to support the Constitution of the United States, shall have engaged in insurrection or rebellion against the same, or given aid or comfort to the enemies thereof. But Congress may by a vote of two-thirds of each House, remove such disability.

SECTION 4. The validity of the public debt of the United States, authorized by law, including debts incurred for payment of pensions and bounties for services in suppressing insurrection or rebellion, shall not be questioned. But neither the United States nor any State shall assume or pay any debt or obligation incurred in aid of insurrection or rebellion against the United States, or any claim for the loss or emancipation of any slave; but all such debts, obligations and claims shall be held illegal and void.

SECTION 5. The Congress shall have power to enforce, by appropriate legislation, the provisions of this article.

ARTICLE XV.[8]

SECTION 1. The right of citizens of the United States to vote shall not be denied or abridged by the United States or by any State on account of race, color, or previous condition of servitude.—

SECTION 2. The Congress shall have power to enforce this article by appropriate legislation.—

[8] Proclaimed to be in force March 30, 1870.

APPENDIX

ARTICLE XVI.[9]

The Congress shall have power to lay and collect taxes on incomes, from whatever source derived, without apportionment among the several States, and without regard to any census or enumeration.

ARTICLE XVII.[10]

The Senate of the United States shall be composed of two Senators from each State, elected by the people thereof, for six years; and each Senator shall have one vote. The electors in each State shall have the qualifications requisite for electors of the most numerous branch of the State legislatures.

When vacancies happen in the representation of any State in the Senate, the executive authority of such State shall issue writs of election to fill such vacancies: *Provided,* That the legislatures of any State may empower the executive thereof to make temporary appointment until the people fill the vacancies by election as the legislature may direct.

This amendment shall not be so construed as to affect the election or term of any Senator chosen before it becomes valid as part of the Constitution.

[9] Proclaimed to be in force, February 25, 1913.
[10] Proclaimed to be in force, May 31, 1913.

INDEX

Accounts of public receipts and expenditures ordered..........188
Acts of Congress, see Congress, and Supreme law.
Adams, John 39
Adams, John Quincy 83, 201
Address to accompany Constitution....................181, 183
Admission of new states, 49, 70, 80, 109, 110, 127, 132, 143,
    144, 182, 205.
Agreements between states, see States, restrictions upon.
Alliances between states, see States, restrictions upon.
Ambassadors 131, 155, 161, 165
Amendments to Articles of Confederation, see Articles of
    Confederation.
Amendments to Constitution, 51, 70, 80, 127, 158, 179, 180, 181,
    189, 190, 191; text of subsequent, see appendix, 252-259.
American People, see People of the United States.
Annapolis Trade Convention, 1786....8, 9, 11, 12, 14, 18, 25, 29, 42
Appointment, power of, see Executive, and President.
Army 49, 147, 161
Articles of association for encouraging economy..............186
Articles of Confederation, framing and adoption of, 2, 3, 25,
    82; government under, 1, 3, 4, 7, 8, 9, 10, 24, 42-52, 153,
    204; amendments to, 4, 5, 7, 11, 51; revision of, the purpose
    of federal convention, 14, 28, 42ff, 69, 72, 73, 128, 191, 201
    (see also under the names of individual states "appoint-
    ment of delegates"); use of, in work of federal convention,
    10, 11, 77, 85, 107, 127, 128, 129, 139-140, 146, 153-154,
    157-158, 190, 208-210; text of, see appendix, 211-224. See
    also Congress of the Confederation, Defects of the Confed-
    eration, and States.
Assumption of state debts............................141, 176
Attainder, bills of...................................147, 154

Baldwin, Abraham, of Georgia, delegate to federal convention,
    26; changes vote on equality in senate, 96-97; member of
    compromise committee, 98; quoted, 162, 181.
Bancroft, George, cited............................106, 145
Bank, establishment of......................46, 189, 202, 204

INDEX

Bankruptcy 48, 14ı

Bassett, Richard, of Delaware, delegate to federal convention..26

Bedford, Gunning, of Delaware, delegate to federal convention, 25; opposed a strong national government, 81; favored equal vote in senate, 96; member of compromise committee, 98; favored compromise on representation, 99.

Bill of rights 185

Bills of credit 147, 153, 154

Blacks, see Slavery.

Blair, John, of Virginia, delegate to federal convention, 16; voted against overruling veto by two-thirds vote, 184.

Blount, William, of North Carolina, delegate to federal convention 24

Brearley, David, of New Jersey, delegate to federal convention, 18, 19; opposed to proportional representation, 75; opposed to a strong national government, 81; made suggestion regarding amendments to Constitution, 190.

British, see Great Britain.

Broom, Jacob, of Delaware, delegate to federal convention......26

Butler, Pierce, of South Carolina, delegate to federal convention, 31; opposed to a strong national government, 81; favored restrictions on foreigners, 137.

Cabal 170

Cabinet, see Executive departments.

Canada, acquisition of, referred to.........................144

Canals, power to construct.................................189

Capitation tax 146, 188

Carroll, Charles, of Carrollton of Maryland, declined appointment to federal convention.............................35

Carroll, Daniel, of Maryland, delegate to federal convention, 36; supported change in ratio of representation, 193.

Caswell, Richard, of North Carolina, declined appointment to federal convention 23

Caucus 62, 63, 152, 153

Census 102-104

Chesapeake Bay 8, 36

Citizenship, requirement of....................123, 130, 137, 165

Clark, Abraham, of New Jersey, failed to attend federal convention 19

INDEX

Clymer, George, of Pennsylvania, delegate to federal convention, 20

Coercion 51, 70, 77, 85, 209

Coles, Edward 60

Columbia College 34

Commander-in-chief of Army and Navy......................161

Commerce, under the Confederation, 5, 7, 12; power to regulate, 85, 140, 147, 152, 208; see also Trade.

Commercial interests.............................109, 148, 210

Committee of Detail, 122, 123, 124-133; report of, 126ff, 143, 155, 157, 163, 177; report of considered, 134-179; importance of work of, 124, 132, 201.

Committee of the Whole House........71ff, 81, 82, 84, 86ff, 91, 123

Committee of Style and Arrangement, 179, 181, 182, 186, 187, 190, 201, 209.

Committee on assumption of state debts.................141, 142

Committee on encouraging economy..........................186

Committee on navigation acts and the slave trade............149

Committee on numbers in first house of representatives...100, 101

Committee on rules.......................................56, 57

Committee on unfinished parts of Constitution............164, 176

Committee to devise a compromise on representation..........97ff

Common defence, see General welfare.

Compromises in federal convention, 100, 135, 183, 201, 203; on inferior courts, 80; on representation, 91-112, 113, 114, 122, 134, 146; on numbers in first house of representatives, 101; on slave trade and navigation acts, 149-152; on election of of president, 166ff; on assumption of state debts, 141, 177; see also Large states.

Confederation, see Articles of Confederation, Commerce, Congress of the Confederation, Defects of the Confederation, and "Federal."

Congress of the Confederation, 2, 3, 4, 5, 8, 10, 11, 24, 54, 82; resolution of, authorizing federal convention, 11, 28, 29, 31; see also Defects of the Confederation.

Congress of the United States, composition and organization of, 50, 69, 74ff, 92, 127, 129, 130, 136, 137, 160-161; members of, 50, 75, 76, 77, 91, 92, 130, 135, 136, 137, 187-188, 189; powers of, 50, 69, 70, 77, 80, 85, 127, 128, 129, 130, 139ff, 145, 147, 153, 154, 158, 161, 176, 186, 187, 189, 203 (see also under headings for separate powers); see also

House of Representatives, Proportional representation, Senate, and Supreme law.

Connecticut, charter and constitution of, 13; appointment of delegates from, to federal convention, 33, 35 (see also under names of delegates); in the opposition in federal convention, 82, 85, 153; voted against a national government, 73; voted against proportional representation, 75, 95; favored equal vote in senate, 95, 96; voted for census of three-fifths of slaves, 103; favored compromise on representation, 104, 106; voted in favor of proposal for payment of debts, 177.

Constitution of the United States, ratification of, 10, 11, 14, 28, 51, 70, 71, 80, 81, 121, 127, 157, 158, 159, 180, 190; agreed to in federal convention, 191; engrossed, 191, 192; signed, 194; description of completed, 191, 200ff, 209, 210; adoption of, 142, 207; success of, 208; text of, see appendix, 233-251; see also Address to accompany Constitution, Amendments to Constitution, Articles of Confederation, Compromises, Defects of the Confederation, Federal Convention, States, and Supreme law.

Contracts, obligation of.............................154, 188
Convention, see Annapolis, and Federal Convention.
Copyright 48, 179
Council of revision, 50, 70, 79, 157, 202; see also Executive council, and Veto.
Courts, see Judiciary.
Credentials, see Federal convention, and separate states.
Credit, see Bills of credit.
Criminal trials, see Judiciary.
Criminals, extradition of...................................157
Currency, see Money.
Cutler, Manasseh, cited 54

Dana, Francis, of Massachusetts, failed to attend federal convention 31
Davie, William R., of North Carolina, delegate to federal convention, 23; member of compromise committee, 98.
Dayton, Jonathan, of New Jersey, delegate to federal convention, 19; favored equal vote in senate, 96.
Debts, see Assumption of state debts.

INDEX

Declaration of Independence, 1, 2; signers of, 17, 18, 20, 21, 25, 32, 34.

Declaration of rights, see Bill of rights.

Defects of the Confederation, 4, 5, 7, 8, 9, 10, 12, 28, 42-52, 68-69, 72, 202ff; object of federal convention to remedy, 9, 10, 23, 28, 42-52, 69, 72, 90, 127-128, 191, 201ff; see also Federal Convention.

Delaware, appointment of delegates from, to federal convention, 11, 24, 56, 75 (see also under names of delegates); voted in favor of national government, 73; voted against three-fifths rule, 75; voted for New Jersey plan, 89; voted against proportional representation in lower house, 95; voted for counting slaves equally with whites, 102; voted against census of free inhabitants, 103; voted for compromise on representation, 104, 105; voted against compromise on slave trade, 150; voted against substituting house of representatives for senate in election of president, 169; in the opposition in federal convention, 73, 82, 85, 153; referred to, 8, 13, 25, 100, 117.

Delegates, see Federal Convention, and under names of individual states.

Departments, see Executive departments.

Detail, committee of, see Committee of Detail.

Dickinson, John, of Delaware, delegate to federal convention, 25; opposed a strong national government, 81; favored popular election of executive, 116; favored restrictions on money-bills, 139; favored council for president, 171-172; part taken by, in work of federal convention, 200; quoted, 204.

Direct taxation, see Taxation.

Dred Scott case..144

Duties on imports, 4, 5, 45, 85, 150, 152, 153, 154; see also Revenue, Taxation.

Duvall, Gabriel, of Maryland, declined appointment to federal convention 35

Education 48, 202

Electors, see Executive, and President.

Elliot, Jonathan, cited......................................47

Ellsworth, Oliver, of Connecticut, delegate to federal conven-

tion, 34, 35; opposed a strong national government, 81;
favored New Jersey plan, 86; member of compromise
committee, 98; makes motion for equal vote in senate, 106;
favored ratification of Constitution by state legislature,
121; member of committee of detail, 122, 124; opposed
restrictions on money-bills, 139; part taken by, in the work
of federal convention, 124, 132, 200; quoted, 93, 132, 149.

Embargo of 1807 206
England, see Great Britain.
Equity, see Judiciary.
Ex post facto laws.....................................147, 154
Execution of the laws of the union, 140, 209, see also Executive,
and President.

Executive, character of, 3, 73, 78, 79, 85, 117, 127, 129, 161, 169-
170, 203; to be single or plural, 50, 77, 85, 160; election of,
70, 77, 78, 85, 88, 115, 117; term of office of, 77, 78, 88, 115,
117; powers and duties of, 79, 85, 86, 88, 119, 157, 160
(see also Veto); see also Impeachment, and President.

Executive council, 50, 166, 171, 172; see also Council of revision.
Executive departments 166, 172
Expenditures, accounts of, ordered...........................188
Experience, importance of, in work of federal convention....
                              52, 128, 129, 203, 204, 205
Exports, prohibition of tax on.................132, 148, 151, 186
Extradition of criminals....................................157

"Federal," meaning of term in federal convention....69 note 1, 84
Federal Convention, calling of, 9, 10, 12, 28, 68; organization
and sessions of, 54-61, 64, 98, 113, 122, 134, 179, 191, 192,
194, 198 (see also Committee of the Whole House); spirit
and purpose of, 62, 63, 81, 84, 94, 114, 118, 134, 185, 187
(see also Compromises, and Defects of the Confederation); delegates to, 10, 14-40, 43, 56, 57, 58, 61, 63, 122
(see also under names of individuals); powers of, 73, 74,
86, 87, 113; reports and proceedings of, 58-60, 65, 110, 194;
a second, proposed, 180-181, 191, 192.

Federal ratio, see Three-fifths rule.
"Federalist," the, quoted....................................203
Felony, see Judiciary.
Few, William, of Georgia, delegate to federal convention......26

INDEX

Finance, see Duties, Money, Money-bills, Revenue, Taxation.

First branch, see Congress of the United States, and House of Representatives.

Fitzsimons, Thomas, of Pennsylvania, delegate to federal convention 21

Force, see Coercion.

Ford, P. L., *Pamphlets on Constitution of United States*.......40

Foreign relations, 47, 50; see also Treaties.

Foreigners 39, 50, 137

France, representative of, cited..........................9, 35, 38

Franklin, Benjamin, of Pennsylvania, delegate to federal convention, 22; and the presidency of the convention, 55; supported a strong national government, 81; made motion for prayers in convention, 94; proposed compromise, 96; member of committee on representation, 98; favored impeachment, 118; favored restrictions on money-bills, 139; supported council for president, 171-172; wanted power granted to construct canals, 189; presented form of approval for Constitution, 192; part taken by, in work of federal convention, 199; quoted, 92, 194.

Franklin, Temple, candidate for secretary of convention.......56

Freedom of the press......................................189

Frontier, see Admission of new states, and the West.

Fugitive slaves 152

Gallatin, Albert 182

General welfare 176-178, 182

Georgia, appointment of delegates from, to federal convention, 11, 26 (see also under names of delegates); one of the large states, 74, 97; divided on equal vote in senate, 96; demanded blacks be counted equally with whites, 102; voted against census of free inhabitants, 103; voted for census of three-fifths of slaves, 103; voted against compromise on representation, 105; favored slave trade, 149, 150; voted for power to construct canals, 189; referred to, 13, 117, 153.

Gerry, Elbridge, of Massachusetts, delegate to federal convention, 32; favored election of members of congress by state legislatures, 75; opposed popular ratification of Constitution, 80, 121, 180; supported a strong national

INDEX

government, 81; member of committee on representation, 98; opposed popular election of executive, 116; favored impeachment, 118; favored restrictions on money-bills, 139, 172; favored assumption of state debts, 141; attended extra-conventional meetings, 153; opposed easy amendment of constitution, 180, 190; favored overruling of veto by two-thirds vote, 183-184; moved for a committee to prepare bill of rights, 185; opposed constitution, 142, 192, 194; part taken by, in work of federal convention, 200; quoted, 117, 157.

Gilman, Nicholas, of New Hampshire, delegate to federal convention 31

Gorham, Nathaniel, of Massachusetts, delegate to federal convention, 32; chairman of committee of the whole, 72; opposed choosing of judiciary by senate, 119; favored popular ratification of Constitution, 121; a member of committee of detail, 122, 124; desired Prince Henry of Prussia to become monarch of the United States, 174; favored election of treasurer by congress, 188; favored change in ratio of representation, 193; part taken by, in work of federal convention, 124, 199; quoted, 100, 109, 110, 136; referred to, 63.

Great Britain 1, 6, 43, 87, 139, 147, 148
Grigsby, H. B., *History of Virginia Convention of 1788*....15, 46

Habeas corpus 156
Hamilton, Alexander, of New York, delegate to federal convention, 29, 94; in Annapolis convention, 9; anecdote of, 22; favored national government, 73, 87; presented his own plan of government, 87; disapproved New Jersey plan, 87; favored British government, 87; charged with favoring monarchy, 88; opposed motion for prayers, 95; member of committee of style, 179; favored approval of Constitution by congress, 180; opposed overruling of veto by two-thirds vote, 183-184; established a national bank, 204; part taken by, in work of federal convention, 87, 94, 197, 206; quoted, 61, 95; referred to, 52, 63.

Harrison, Robert Hanson, of Maryland, declined appointment to federal convention.....................................35
Hazard, W. P., *Annals of Philadelphia*..............173-174 note

INDEX

Henry, Patrick, of Virginia, declined appointment to federal
    convention, 15; referred to, 17.
Henry, Prince of Prussia, suggested as monarch of the United
    States 174
History, use of, in federal convention....................52, 203
House of Representatives, election of members of, 69, 75, 76,
    92; term and payment of members of, 76, 91, 131, 138;
    qualifications for members of, 123, 130, 135, 137; number
    of members in first, 100, 101, 105; substituted for senate
    in eventual election of president, 168; see also Congress of
    the United States, Impeachment, Money-bills, and Pro-
    portional representation.
Houston, William C., of New Jersey, delegate to federal con-
    vention 18
Houstoun, William, of Georgia, delegate to federal convention..27

Impeachment 70, 79, 86, 118, 130, 131, 160, 161, 166, 172, 203
Import duties, see Duties on imports.
Independence Hall 54
Independent Gazetteer, quoted.........................173 note
Indian Queen, a tavern......................................62
Indians, policy in dealing with.............................48
Ingersoll, Jared, of Pennsylvania, delegate to federal con-
    vention 21
Insurrections 140
Internal improvements 49, 189, 202, 204
International Law, see Law of nations.
Inventions 48

Jackson, William, elected secretary of federal convention.......56
Jay, John, quoted 43
Jefferson, Thomas 39, 42, 43, 46, 74
Jenifer, Daniel of St. Thomas, of Maryland, delegate to federal
    convention 36, 96
Johnson, William Samuel, of Connecticut, delegate to federal
    convention, 33; introduced subject of compromise on
    representation, 106; member of committee of style, 179;
    seconded motion for committee on economy, 186, 187; part
    taken by, in work of federal convention, 200; quoted, 89,
    134.

INDEX

Jones, Willie, of North Carolina, declined appointment to
    federal convention 23

Judiciary, appointment and term of, 70, 79, 119, 155, 165;
    organization of, 3, 50, 70, 73, 79, 80, 86, 127, 154, 155;
    jurisdiction of, 4, 47, 50, 70, 79, 86, 119, 120, 130, 131, 154,
    155, 156, 185, 202, 209; right of, in cases of unconstitu-
    tional laws, 120, 156; see also Council of revision, and
    Veto.

Jury trials 131, 156, 185

King, Rufus, of Massachusetts, delegate to federal convention,
    32; favored popular ratification of constitution, 80, 121;
    supported a strong national government, 81; opposed
    equal vote in senate, 96; favored popular election of execu-
    tive, 116; opposed impeachment, 118; proposed clause on
    obligation of contracts, 154, 188; member of committee of
    style, 179, 188; favored appointment of treasurer by con-
    gress, 188; supported change in ratio of representation,
    193; quoted, 108, 157, 167, 172; part taken by, in work of
    federal convention, 199.

Krauel, Richard, cited 174

Langdon, John, of New Hampshire, delegate to federal con-
    vention 37

Lansing, John, of New York, delegate to federal convention,
    29; voted with Yates against Hamilton, 73, 197; opposed
    strong national government, 81; favored New Jersey plan,
    86; left convention, 105.

Large states vs. small states in federal convention, 57, 82, 91,
    101, 111, 113, 116, 118, 166, 168; see also Compromises.

Laurens, Henry, of South Carolina, failed to attend federal
    convention 31

Laurens, John 56

Law of nations 46, 47, 140

Lee, Richard Henry, declined to serve in federal convention....16

Lee, Thomas Sim, of Maryland, declined appointment to
    federal convention 35

Legal tender 153, 154

Legislature, see Congress.

INDEX

Letter to Congress, see Address to accompany Constitution.

Livingston, Henry W., letter of Morris to....................144

Livingston, William, governor of New Jersey, delegate to federal convention 19

Louisiana purchase 144

Lower house, see House of Representatives.

McClurg, James, of Virginia, delegate to federal convention....16

McHenry, James, of Maryland, delegate to federal convention, 35, 152; notes of proceedings kept by, 152, 174, 193; favored power in congress to erect piers, 178; voted against overruling veto by two-thirds vote, 184.

Madison, James, of Virginia, delegate to federal convention, 17, 63; delegate to Annapolis convention, 8; favored a national bank, 46; favored popular election of members of congress, 76; opposed election of senate by state legislatures, 76; favored popular ratification of constitution, 80, 121; opposed New Jersey plan, 86, 90; opposed equal vote in senate, 96; opposed compromise on representation, 97, 99; favored popular election of executive, 116; favored impeachment, 118; opposed choosing of judiciary by senate, 119; objected to ratio of representation, 136; approved May as time of meeting of congress, 136; suggested another standard of value than money, 138; opposed restrictions on money-bills, 139; opposed limitation on admission of new states, 143; suggested permitting of export taxes by two-thirds vote, 148; favored ratification of constitution by seven states, 158; supported a council for president, 171-172; member of committee of style, 179; opposed overruling of veto by two-thirds vote, 183-184; favored power to incorporate, 189; notes of debates kept by, 59, 60, 64, 66; quoted, 7, 17, 52, 61, 93, 98, 110, 111, 113, 114, 117, 121, 139, 145, 157, 167, 172, 177, 181, 191, 199, 208; part taken by, in work of federal convention, 68, 81, 196, 198, 200, 206.

Manufactures, committee appointed to report articles of association for encouraging 186

Maritime cases 86, 155, 185

Marque and reprisal 153

Marshall, John 43

INDEX

Martin, Alexander, of North Carolina, delegate to federal convention 23

Martin, Luther, of Maryland, delegate to federal convention, 36; opposed a strong national government, 81; in the opposition in federal convention, 85, 153, 200; speech by, 93; cast Maryland's vote in favor of equality in senate, 96; member of compromise committee, 98; proposed supreme law clause, 120, 209; part taken by, in work of federal convention, 200; quoted, 66, 81, 96-97, 153, 157, 174.

Maryland, appointment of delegates from, to federal convention, 35 (see also under names of delegates); trade agreement of, with Virginia, 8, 36; in the opposition in federal convention, 73, 82; divided on proportional representation, 75, 95; voted against proportional representation in upper house, 75; divided on New Jersey plan, 89; voted against census of free inhabitants, 103; voted for compromise on representation, 105; against voting per capita in senate, 122; obtained uniformity of commerce regulations, 152; voted for overruling president's veto by two-thirds vote, 184; referred to, 13, 137.

Mason, George, of Virginia, delegate to federal convention, 17, 63; favored popular election of members of congress, 76; supported a strong national government, 81; member of compromise committee on representation, 98; opposed popular election of executive, 116; favored impeachment, 118; favored popular ratification of constitution, 121; favored restrictions on money-bills, 139, 172; opposed limitation on admission of new states, 143; objected to recognition of slavery, 149; attended extra-conventional meetings, 153; favored council for president, 171-172; favored overruling veto by two-thirds vote, 184; consented to no action on jury in civil cases, 185; favored bill of rights, 185; proposed modification on prohibition of exports, 186; favored a second convention, 191-192; opposed Constitution, 191-192, 194; quoted, 56, 74, 116, 157, 167, 168, 186; part taken by, in work of federal convention, 199.

Massachusetts, appointment of delegates from, to federal convention, 31; favored a strong national government, 73, 82; divided on compromise on representation, 105; voted against impeachment, 118; voted for negative on state laws, 120; constitution of, furnished model for veto, 145; voted for prohibition of export taxes, 148; referred to, 13, 101, 108, 117.

Mercer, John Francis, of Maryland, delegate to federal convention, 36; list made by, of those favoring monarchy, 174.

Middle states 147, 148

Mifflin, Thomas, of Pennsylvania, delegate to federal convention, 20

Militia 49, 140, 142, 209

Monarchy 77, 88, 162, 173, 174

Money 45-46, 108, 138, 147, 153, 154

Money-bills 99, 106, 138, 172

Montesquieu 49

Morris, Gouverneur, of Pennsylvania, delegate to federal convention, 21; anecdote of, 22; opposed equal voting in federal convention, 57; supported a strong national government, 81; opposed compromise on representation, 99; proposed clause on taxation and representation, 103, 104; member of committees, 109, 177, 179, 181; favored popular election of executive, 116; opposed impeachment, 118; favored impeachment, 118; favored popular ratification of constitution, 121; opposed restrictions on money-bills, 139, 172-173; favored limitation on admission of new states, 143, 205; favored prohibition of paper money, 147; favored assumption of debts, 177-178; opposed overruling of veto by two-thirds vote, 183-184; proposed provision in Constitution limiting amendments, 190; devised form for approval of Constitution, 192; part taken by, in work of federal convention, 109, 177-178, 181, 183, 198, 199, 201; quoted, 62, 66, 94, 144, 150, 157, 167, 172, 178, 205.

Morris, Robert, of Pennsylvania, delegate to federal convention 20, 37, 55, 206

"National" 73, 91

National peace and harmony 119, 155

Naturalization 48, 140

Navigation acts 6, 132, 148, 149-151, 188

Navy 49, 141

Negative on state laws 51, 70, 77, 88, 120, 202

Neilson, John, of New Jersey, declined appointment to federal convention 19

Nelson, Thomas, of Virginia, declined appointment to federal
convention 16

New England 147, 148, 151

New Hampshire, appointment of delegates from, to federal
convention, 11, 37, 96, 123; referred to, 13, 101, 117.

New Jersey, appointment of delegates from, to federal convention, 11, 18 (see also under names of delegates); in
the opposition in federal convention, 73, 82, 113, 153; voted
against proportional representation, 75, 95; voted against
three-fifths rule, 75; voted for New Jersey plan, 89; proposed that New Hampshire be urged to attend, 96; voted
for compromise on representation, 104; voted against compromise on slave trade, 150; referred to, 7, 13, 100.

New Jersey Plan, 84-90, 107, 113, 123, 125, 128, 141; text of,
see appendix, 229-232.

New York, presented resolution in congress authorizing federal
convention, 28; appointment of delegates from, to federal
convention, 29 (see also under names of delegates); in
the opposition in federal convention, 73, 82, 85; vote of,
divided on a national government, 73; voted for New
Jersey plan, 89; voted against proportional representation,
95; referred to, 5, 7, 100, 105, 189; constitution of, 13, 29,
129, 161.

Newspapers, quoted 23, 114, 173, 174, 195

Nobility 146, 153

North Carolina, appointment of delegates from, to federal
convention, 11, 22 (see also under names of delegates);
voted in favor of national government, 73; voted for
census of three-fifths of slaves, 103; voted for compromise
on representation, 105; voted for negative on state laws,
120; favored slave trade, 149; proposal for an additional
member from, in first congress, 189; referred to, 7, 13, 109,
150.

North vs. South 108, 110, 111, 149, 150

Nullification 206

Oath, to support constitution 70, 127

Office-holders, limitations on....................50, 135, 136, 146

Opposition, the, in federal convention......................
73, 82, 84, 92, 134, 187, 188, 200

INDEX

Ordinance of 1787 154
Osnaburgh, Bishop of 173
Otto, French *chargé d'affaires*, see France.
Oxford University 31, 33

Patents 179
Paterson, William, of New Jersey, delegate to federal convention, 18; a leader of the opposition, 75, 81; presented New
 Jersey plan, 84; favored New Jersey plan, 86; member of
 committee on representation, 98; opposed compromise
 report on representation, 100; on the powers of federal
 convention, 113; favored popular election of executive,
 116; favored ratification of Constitution by state legislatures, 121; part taken by, in work of federal convention,
 200.
Paterson Resolutions, see New Jersey Plan.
Pendleton, Nathaniel, of Georgia, declined appointment to federal convention 26
Pennsylvania, appointment of delegates from, to federal convention, 11, 20, 24; opposed voting by states in federal
 convention, 57; favored a strong national government,
 73, 82; voted against compromise on representation, 105;
 favored proportional representation, 111; voted for popular election of executive, 116; voted against compromise
 on slave trade, 150; voted for power to construct canals,
 189; referred to, 8, 13, 25, 100, 109, 117.
Pennsylvania Packet and Daily Advertiser, quoted...........195
Penn, William, quoted 209
People of the United States.........2, 52, 74, 190, 191, 198, 210
Personal influence in federal convention.................63ff, 198
Philadelphia, 7, 10, 11, 12, 23, 54, 189; College of, referred to, 24
Pickering, John, of New Hampshire, failed to attend federal
 convention 38
Pickering, Timothy, letter of Morris to......................181
Pierce, William, of Georgia, delegate to federal convention,
 27; character sketches of delegates by, quoted, 16-38
 passim.
Pinckney, Charles, of South Carolina, delegate to federal convention, 30, 63; presented his plan of government, 71;
 favored election of members of congress by state legis-

latures, 75, 92; favored ratification of Constitution by less than unanimous vote of states, 81; supported a strong national government, 81; criticised New Jersey's motives, 113; opposed popular election of executive, 116; opposed impeachment, 118; opposed restrictions on money-bills, 139; favored overruling of veto by two-thirds vote, 183-184; part taken by, in work of federal convention, 199; see also Pinckney Plan.

Pinckney, Charles Cotesworth, of South Carolina, delegate to federal convention, 31; favored election of members of congress by state legislatures, 75; supported a strong national government, 81; proposed compromise committee on representation, 97; explained slave trade compromise, 151; part taken by, in work of federal convention, 199.

Pinckney Plan 71, 72, 83, 123, 126, 128, 129

Piracy, trial of 4, 47

Popular elections, see Congress, Constitution, Executive, House of Representatives, President, and Senate.

Population, see Census, Proportional representation, and Wealth.

Powers of congress, see Congress of the United States, powers of.

Preamble to Constitution 190, 191

President, office of, 129, 131, 161, 163, 165; election and term of, 160-172; powers and duties of, 129, 160-163, 165, 166, 171, 172; see also Executive, Impeachment, and Monarchy.

Princeton College 18

Property qualifications 123, 130, 135

Proportional representation ....
50, 69, 74, 75, 82, 84, 92, 94-112, 136, 193

Randolph, Edmund, of Virginia, delegate to federal convention, 16; delegate to Annapolis convention, 8; presented Virginia Plan, 68, 71, 202; opposed single executive, 77; supported a strong national government, 81; opposed New Jersey Plan, 86; proposed a census, 101-102; opposed popular election of executive, 116; favored impeachment, 118; favored popular ratification of Constitution, 121; member of committee of detail, 122, 124, 125, 132; favored restrictions on money-bills, 139; objected to Constitution,

180, 191, 194; voted in favor of overruling veto by two-thirds vote, 184; favored a second convention, 180-181, 191; part taken by, in work of federal convention, 124, 199.

Randolph Resolutions, see Virginia Plan.

Read, George, of Delaware, delegate to federal convention, 25, 147

Receipts and expenditures 188

Representation, see Congress, House of Representatives, Proportional representation.

Republican party, see Democratic-Republican party.

Requisitions 4, 5, 45, 85

Restrictions, see Congress, and States.

Revenue, 4, 5, 45, 70, 85, 86, 152; see also Duties, Money, Money-bills, and Taxation.

Revolution, the....1, 15, 19, 20, 23, 27, 29, 31, 34, 35, 38, 39, 109

Rhode Island 5, 11, 13, 117, 188

Rutledge, John, of South Carolina, delegate to federal convention, 30, 63; conducted Washington to the chair, 55; moved to take up proportional representation, 93; member of compromise committee on representation, 98; opposed popular election of executive, 116; as a member of committee of detail, 122, 124, 125, 126, 132; opposed restrictions on money-bills, 139; part taken by, in work of federal convention, 124, 199.

Seat of government 48, 179, 189

Secession 205

Second branch, see Senate.

Senate, election and term of members of, 69, 76, 88, 91, 111, 112, 187, 188; voting in, 121, 122; qualifications for members of, 123, 130, 135, 137; powers and privileges of, 119, 131, 165, 167, 168, 169, 171, 172; presiding officer of, 129, 161, 165, 169; see also Congress, and Proportional representation.

Separation of powers 49, 69

Shays's rebellion 49

Sherman, Roger, of Connecticut, delegate to federal convention, 34, 35; favored election of members of congress by state legislatures, 75; opposed popular ratification of constitution, 80; opposed a strong national government, 81; proposal by, in compromise committee, 98; opposed popular election of executive, 116; opposed limitation on admission of new states, 143; explained compromise in election of president, 167; favored provision for payment of debts, 177; member of committee on unfinished parts of constitution, 177; prevented modification of general welfare clause, 183; favored overruling of veto by two-thirds vote, 183-184; opposed bill of rights, 185; made suggestion regarding amendments, 190; part taken by, in work of federal convention, 200.

Slave trade 132, 148, 149-151, 152, 180

Slavery, 102, 103, 110, 148, 152; see also Three-fifths rule.

Small states, in the federal convention, 84, 92, 97, 98, 107, 111, 113, 114, 116, 119, 167, 172; see also Compromises, and Large states.

South, the 108, 110-111, 148

South Carolina, appointment of delegates from, to federal convention, 30, 153 (see also under names of delegates); voted in favor of a national government, 73; demanded blacks be counted equally with whites, 102, 103; voted against compromise on representation, 105; voted against impeachment, 118; favored slave trade, 149, 150, 151; referred to, 7, 13, 109.

Spaight, Richard D., of North Carolina, delegate to federal convention 23

Sparks, Jared, letter of Madison to.........................181

Specie 153, 154

States, under the Articles of Confederation, 1, 3, 7, 8, 24, 46, 47, 48, 82, 145, 208; constitutions and governments of, 1, 13, 128, 129, 130, 139, 186, 203, 204; representation of, in federal convention, 54, 57; relation of, to the new constitution, 70, 71, 120, 158, 180; guarantees to, 49, 70, 80, 127, 132; method of settling disputes between, 128, 131, 155, 156; restrictions upon, 47, 48, 77, 85, 88, 120, 127, 128, 153, 154, 188; rights and privileges of, 69, 79-80, 111, 127, 128, 142, 143, 157, 186, 190, 206; courts of, 80, 86, 155; see also under names of separate states, Admission, Assumption, Large states, Militia, Negative on state laws, Small states.

Stiles, Ezra 162, 181

Stone, Thomas, of Maryland, declined appointment to federal convention 35

INDEX

Strong, Caleb, of Massachusetts, delegate to federal convention 33, 63

Suffrage, see Congress, House of Representatives, and Senate.

Supreme court, see Judiciary.

Supreme law clause 85, 120, 209

Tariff of 1816 206

Taxation, under Articles of Confederation, 7, 12; under Constitution, 45, 85, 103-105, 140, 146, 150, 177, 188, 208; see also Capitation tax, Duties on imports, Exports, and Requisitions.

Territory, control of 145

Three-fifths rule 5, 75, 85, 99, 102-104, 105, 107

Trade, 5, 6, 7, 18, 45, 85, 86, 210; see also Annapolis, Commerce, Commercial Interests, and Congress, powers of.

Treason 48, 140, 146

Treasurer of the United States 188

Treaties, breach of, 46, 77; how to be made, 131, 153, 165, 171; enforcement of, 85, 86, 140, 153, 155 (see also Supreme law).

Treaty of Paris, 1783 ....46, 82

Uniformity 7, 45, 46, 48, 140, 141, 152

University, power to establish 189

University of Georgia 27

Upper house, see Senate.

Veto, 50, 70, 79, 85, 88, 119-120, 145, 156-157, 160, 161, 183-184, 202

Vice-President 165, 169, 203

Virginia, appointment of delegates from, to federal convention, 10, 14-17, 18, 20, 24, 35, 39 (see also under names of delegates); proposed Annapolis trade convention, 8; favored a national government, 73, 82; favored equal voting in federal convention, 57; voted for census of three-fifths of slaves, 103; voted against compromise on representation, 105; opposed election of senators by state legislatures, 111; favored proportional representation, 111; voted for negative on state laws, 120; voted against compromise on slave trade, 150; voted against overruling veto by two-thirds vote, 184; voted for power to construct canals, 189; referred to, 7, 8, 13, 15, 17, 36, 46, 109, 117, 168, 185.

INDEX

Virginia Plan, 68-73, 82, 84-86, 88, 89, 91, 107, 113, 115, 122, 202; text of, see appendix, 225-228.

Voting, see Congress, Federal Convention, House of Representatives, Proportional representation, and Senate.

Walton, George, of Georgia, declined to attend federal convention 26

War 141, 153

War of 1812 ....59, 204

Washington, George, of Virginia, delegate to federal convention, 15; anecdotes of, 64, 65, 66, 74; supported a strong national government, 81; voted for restrictions on money-bills, 139, favored ratification of constitution by seven states, 158; voted against overruling veto by two-thirds vote, 184; favored change in ratio of representation, 193; favored internal improvements, 204; part taken by, in work of federal convention, 55, 64-66, 132, 163, 198; quoted, 21, 43, 163, 194; referred to, 36, 94.

Watson, John F., *Annals of Philadelphia* ....55, 173-174 note

Wealth 101, 102

Weather during federal convention 93, 104, 134

Webster, Pelatiah 53

Welfare, see General welfare.

West, Benjamin, of New Hampshire, failed to attend federal convention 38

West, the, 48-49, 108, 109, 110, 143, 145, 204; see also Admission of new states.

William and Mary College 17

Williamson, Hugh, of North Carolina, delegate to federal convention, 24; explained why prayers were not read in convention, 95; opposed compromise report on representation, 100; suggested modification in taking of census, 102; favored restrictions on money-bills, 139; member of committee on unfinished parts of constitution, 184; obtained change in provisions concerning veto, 183-185; favored provision for jury in civil cases, 184-185; quoted, 169.

Wilson, James, of Pennsylvania, delegate to federal convention, 21; favored popular election of members of congress, 76; favored popular election of executive, 78, 115; favored popular ratification of Constitution, 80, 121; favored ratification of Constitution by less than unanimous vote of states, 81; favored a strong national government, 81; opposed New Jersey plan, 86; opposed equal vote in senate, 96; opposed compromise committee on representation, 97; favored impeachment, 118; opposed choosing of judiciary by senate, 119; as a member of committee of detail, 122, 124, 125, 126, 198, 201; opposed restrictions on foreigners, 137; opposed restrictions on money-bills, 139; supported council for president, 171-172; proposed amendment of Constitution by two-thirds of states, 180; read Franklin's speeches, 199; part taken by, in work of federal convention, 124, 181, 197, 198, 200, 201, 206; quoted, 62, 157, 164.

Wolcott, Erastus, of Connecticut, declined appointment to federal convention 33

Wythe, George, of Virginia, delegate to federal convention......17

Yale 27

Yates, Robert, of New York, delegate to federal convention, 29; opposed a strong national government, 73, 81; in opposition to Hamilton, 197; member of compromise committee, 98; left federal convention, 105; quoted, 93, 98.